THE OPTIMIST'S

MANIFESTO

AN OPTIMIST'S GUIDE TO LIVING IN THE REAL WORLD

ELIZABETH SHAW

Elizabeth Shaw

THE OPTIMIST'S MANIFESTO

Printed in the United States of America.

First Printing, 2018

ISBN 978-1-7325365-0-0

Library of Congress Control Number: 2018908419

www.Davine.com

This book is dedicated to my parents
for raising me to be an optimist.

To my father, for teaching me to believe in possibility
and showing me that nothing is impossible.

To my mother, for leading by example with what it
means to believe the best: in myself, in others,
and in the world.

I am an optimist because of both of you, and for that
I am eternally grateful.

CONTENTS

THE OPTIMIST'S MANIFESTO

INTRODUCTION

THE OPTIMISM SUPERPOWER

The irony of the fact that I started writing a book on optimism during one of the most difficult seasons of my life is not lost on me.

Since I was a young girl, I've been told that I'm a hopeless optimist. Of course, I take issue with the "hopeless" part of that sentiment, but if you think of it in relation to being a "hopeless romantic" I suppose I understand the notion. Optimism is my default way of operating. I am an eternal optimist, and even in the darkest moments, I am always looking for the light.

The season of my life when I began – really began – writing this book seemed to be the universe's way of reinforcing the lessons I've espoused my entire life. During this time, my optimism also became much more practical. Instead of defaulting to this mindset, which can be difficult when you are in the midst of crisis, my optimism grew roots – grounding me in action which could reinforce those beliefs, even when the feelings weren't easily there; and inspiring me to move forward in difficult and challenging times.

Practical optimism for inspired living. This is how I began referring to the steps, tricks, and tools I picked up along the way. They are my secret arsenal that have helped me maintain my optimism even when I've wanted to give up, give in, and dismiss this core part of myself.

Perhaps you have picked up this book because you are also an optimist and want to celebrate that part of yourself by connecting with, and possibly learning from, other optimists. Or, maybe your optimism has been challenged by the difficult things happening throughout the world, and personally in your own life, and you're questioning whether optimism is still right for you or worth it in the grand scheme of things. It could be that you don't see yourself as an optimist or a pessimist, but you are curious about optimism and open to ideas about how to incorporate optimism into your life.

Whatever your reason for choosing to read this book, my goal is that it will be an encouragement and toolkit for you to live with optimism in every season of life. Through it all, it is possible to live with hope and joy and expectation of the good. And for everyone it looks slightly different.

This book has been built around sharing my tried and true perspectives of how to maintain optimism in a very realistic and often pessimistic world. I've included my secret arsenal of tips, tricks and mindsets that have helped optimism become my superpower. There are tangible steps to achieve optimism, tools for implementing practical optimism in your own life, and reflective questions along the way. We will be having a dialogue about optimism. I encourage you to keep a notepad or journal on hand to write down action steps that resonate with you, and to answer the reflective questions that will help you define and apply optimism for yourself.

Although I have always embraced optimism as my most defining characteristic, it's taken me a long time to clearly be able to define it. In many ways, it's easier to define optimism by what it is not.

Here are a few things I've learned about what optimism is not:

* Optimism is not happiness. While these states often go hand in hand, being happy does not equate to being optimistic, and vice versa. It's entirely possible to be optimistic and unhappy (those dark seasons of my life are proof of that), and it's just as possible to be happy and pessimistic. That said, the most optimistic people are often the happiest, but you don't want to confuse the two.

* Optimism is not unrealistic wishful thinking, all sunshine and roses, or seeing the world through rose colored glasses. Seeing the light in situations is a key component of being optimistic, but this doesn't mean believing in false realities, ignoring negative or difficult situations, or sugar-coating everything.

* Optimism cannot be simplified into seeing the glass as half full as opposed to half empty, or simply as positive thinking. Life is much more complicated than glasses being full or not. Life includes nuances that require quite a bit more detail for a situation to be understood – such as where the glass comes from, what it's filled with, what its purpose may be, and whether it can be refilled. In other words, don't try to make something black and white when the matter is really filled with thousands of shades of gray and color in between.

All of this begs the question, what is optimism?

Mr. Webster defines optimism as:

1. A disposition or tendency to look on the more favorable side of events or conditions and to expect the most favorable outcome.

2. The belief that good ultimately predominates over evil in the world.

3. The belief that goodness pervades reality.

I agree with Mr. Webster in many regards, and have adapted Webster's definition into my own, with a slight variation...

Optimism is the ability to look at a situation, event, or conditions and believe in the possibility of the most favorable outcomes. It is seeing the good in every situation, believing the best of people and the world, and approaching life with hope and possibility. *Practical optimism* is the ability to see the possibility of the most favorable outcomes, and act in a way that moves toward the most favorable outcome becoming a reality.

So, let's put it this way. What you do with the glass is much more important than how you see it.

I see optimism as being a lot like faith. Even if you are wrong, what harm will come if you believe? But if you don't believe and you are wrong, there is much more at stake. Without practicing optimism, you're sacrificing joy and connection and peace in exchange for believing the worst. In the absence of optimism, it is easier to succumb to fear, to feel like you're never enough, and live as though you're always expecting the other shoe to drop. I refuse to do that, and I hope that by picking up this book, you're doing the same.

What would it look like for you if you believed in the best

possible outcomes for yourself? How would that hope, and anticipation of the best, impact your relationships, your work, and your community? Do you believe that optimism has the power to change the world for the better?

In this book we will review the overarching mindset of optimism, and then dive into practical optimism as it relates to key areas of our lives: work, relationships, community, and self. We will then wrap up with what it means to have a worldview that empowers us to live optimistically.

Optimism is my superpower. This is something that I've been told by others, and something that I truly believe, myself. And, specifically, I believe in practical optimism. I don't simply believe in the most favorable side of events, but I take action to shape reality accordingly.

People have suggested that I live a charmed life, blessed with success and breathtaking experiences and amazing community, and that (of course) it is easy to be optimistic when life is charmed. I agree that my life has been blessed, more so than I could possibly deserve, and I am constantly filled with awe and gratitude at the breadth of experiences I've had in my almost 40 years. Perhaps it's natural that people see this life I've built and assume it to be the reason for my optimism... but there's far more to it.

I am not optimistic because of my charmed life. In fact, I think the cause and effect is reversed. My life is charmed because I am so optimistic. Simply put, I have made my own charmed reality because of my mindset and actions. Optimism has given me the courage to take risks, to say YES even when faced with reasons to say NO. It has opened me up to unexpected people along my journey, resulting in some of the most beautiful relationships because I saw the best in someone, instead of expecting the worst of them. There's no doubt also that optimism has furthered the success of my career, because I look for solutions and see benefits when others see problems and failures, and I can take advantage of the lessons learned via such challenges to improve myself and make situations even better.

I'd also argue my own optimism has helped lead to the charmed lives of the people who I love. It makes a difference when a key person in your life sees the best in you, sees all of your potential, and hopes for all of the greatness available to you – it gives you the faith and courage to believe it yourself. So, by being optimistic, know that you're not just helping yourself and building your own charmed life; you're actually building charm into the lives of those around you.

The impact of optimism is not something that is only available to me. Optimism is something that you can cultivate in your own life, and then experience the amazing benefits and transformation as a result of living a life of optimism. Picking up this book is a great first step in furthering your life of optimism and applying practical optimism for a more inspired, fulfilled, and rewarding life.

Optimism is my superpower. Will it be one of yours too?

PART 1

AN OPTIMISTIC MINDSET

"When you're an optimist, life has a funny way of looking after you." – Simon Sinek

Though we often think of optimism as a singular mindset, this way of seeing the world is made up of many smaller beliefs and viewpoints, building together to give us the outlook which we call optimism. I am beginning this book with what I consider to be the key foundations of being optimistic. These are the all-important viewpoints that form the foundation for building optimism in yourself and applying it to your life, the thought processes that create the framework for the action steps outlined in future chapters.

Without these foundational mindsets, it is difficult to sustain optimism, let alone to learn to apply it practically in every area of your life. With these mindsets as your key building blocks, optimism comes with genuine ease and flow, serving as a natural default for how you operate and view the world. Ultimately, this mindset enables you to practice optimism throughout every aspect and every season of your life.

CHAPTER 1

BELIEVE IN POSSIBILITY

"Alice laughed: 'There's no use trying,' she said; 'one can't believe impossible things.' 'I daresay you haven't had much practice,' said the Queen. 'When I was younger, I always did it for half an hour a day. Why, sometimes I've believed as many as six impossible things before breakfast.'"
– Alice in Wonderland

When was the last time you believed in the impossible? In the infinite possibilities of the universe? In the unlimited potential of yourself? Or simply, when you just believed in possibility? Stop and think about it for a minute. You're busy with your day to day life, sure, but if you try, can you believe that tomorrow holds wonderful possibility for you, personally? Do you believe that your dreams are really within your grasp? Can you believe that your deepest desires have potential to become your reality?

Albert Einstein said, "It is better to believe than to disbelieve; in doing so you bring everything to the realm of possibility."

The most important foundation of being optimistic is simply allowing yourself to believe in possibility. To set aside all of the doubts, the uncertainties, the questions, and see what could be possible.

You might be thinking, "Easier said than done", right? Or you're thinking, "Sure, I believe that my dreams can become reality, but how does believing that make it so?" Believing in possibility is the foundation that gives us the courage to take action, to move from the thoughts and desires we carry within ourselves and transform those thoughts into steps moving us towards making those dreams a reality.

I recall the first time that I understood what it meant to really believe in possibility, in a way that prompted action instead of existing only as an idea in my mind.

It was September of 2001, I had just graduated from college and I was bright-eyed, "hopelessly" optimistic, and preparing to move cross-country from Idaho to Boston. And then September 11 happened. I delayed my plans by a few months, but come January 2002, I was still undeterred from my desire to move to Boston – despite the fact that I didn't have a job or an apartment there, and I didn't know a soul in the city. Yet, I could see the possibility. I knew what a life in Boston could look like for me, and I was determined to make it happen.

A few days before my scheduled departure, I was sitting at a table in a cafe with two friends, a few acquaintances, and a local pastor. As I shared my plans for Boston and my dreams of what was in store for me, the pastor pulled out a $1 bill from his wallet. "Boston is a tough, expensive city. It's naive of you to move during this time of recession, without a job, without contacts, and expect to actually succeed." Sliding the $1 bill across the table, he continued, with even more condescension in his voice: "You're going to need all the help you can get. Give me a call when you fail and you've moved back home."

As my face flushed with anger and embarrassment, I fought back the tears, but unfortunately, I didn't have a good response. Other than my own unwavering belief that a job, an apartment, and a great life was possible for me in Boston, I couldn't refute his pessimism. This pessimism, and the "you're out of your mind" attitude towards me, was not unique to that pastor. Other than my parents, everyone thought I was crazy for moving at the time and in the way that I did.

I'd love to say that I proved everyone wrong with the fairytale version of the story... having arrived in Boston to immediately be offered my dream job and secure an amazing apartment and make lifelong friends and live happily ever after. The fairytale isn't usually reality, though. I arrived in Boston to a snowstorm (which served me right for being crazy enough to move in January). The room I'd rented from an online posting was a makeshift space in a living room segmented off by bookshelves that didn't even reach the ceiling or connect in a way that provided any privacy. And, I spent the first few weeks crying in hushed tones in my "room" – full of fear and disappointment over what a mistake I'd made.

But, given some time, and work, and a lot more time, and a lot more work, eventually the pieces started to fall together. Through networking, I found an apartment right in the center of Boston that miraculously fit my modest budget and was within walking distance to things I longed to be close to. After dozens upon dozens of interviews, I eventually landed a job in a field I was interested in pursuing. It wasn't a glamorous job by any means, but it put me on a path to pursuing my dream of being an event planner. A contact had recommended a church for me to check out, a "hot spot" for young people in Boston, and it became a place of community for me during my time of transition and settling in to Boston. And now, 16 years later, Boston is home for me, for my family, for my business, for the community I'm a part of, and for so many of the things that bring me joy and define my life.

This didn't happen because I took the pessimist's advice and decided to do what seemed more realistic – which was to do nothing, staying in Idaho where it was safe and predictable. No. All of this happened because I believed in possibility instead of giving in to doubt, uncertainty, and fear – which so many people were advocating for me to embrace. I believed in the possibility of what my life in Boston could be, and although it's not exactly what I imagined, in so many ways it's better than I ever could have envisioned.

What do you secretly dream about being possible, but have avoided expressing or pursuing because it doesn't seem realistic?

UCLA refers to optimism as a doubt-defying state of mind. This is what it means to believe in possibility. As humans, we are wired for potential, for possibility. We dream big dreams. We hope for the impossible.

Simply, you must allow yourself to dream. Dream small dreams. Dream big dreams. Dream seemingly impossible dreams. Give yourself the freedom to dream as big and high and deep as you possibly can. About anything it is that you want, that you wish could be possible for you. About what you want for your life, for your work, for your family, for your relationships – all of it.

Now, I know you're thinking that it's not that simple. You are thinking that you have bills to pay, and loved ones depending on you, and maybe you don't even believe that what you want is possible. I get it, because I have been there before too. And we will address those items to come. But for now, set aside the doubts and uncertainties that creep in, the inner monologue that says, "be realistic", and the feedback from others that makes you question what is possible.

When building your foundation of optimism, it is not the time to censor your dreams, but to embrace them, giving them space to live and breathe and grow.

In grabbing hold of all that you wish could be possible, the first step is to consider all the ways that your dream could happen. Think about the reality that could make it so. Too often, we default to the few things that could go wrong and end up creating obstacles to reaching what we hope is possible. Instead of allowing yourself to fall into that trap, focus on the dozens or hundreds of ways that things could go right, and all the ways that it could work out.

A wise mentor reminded me once that it's not either/or: there aren't only two ways to reach a goal or two ways to find a solution. Instead, there are infinitely more possibilities for something to come together. Write down at least ten different ways that your dream could become a reality, the various ways that your path can lead to success, in which everything is working in your favor, in which your hard work is paying off, in which the best possible outcomes and the almost best possible outcomes are occurring. You will surprise yourself by the numerous ways your dream can happen, if you let it.

Show yourself the depth of opportunity and ways in which

things can work to bring about amazing possibilities. Imagine how it can all come together by marrying the infinitely possible paths that can take you where you want to go – with what you want to believe is possible.

And, voila, you're believing in possibility.

Questions for Reflection:

What does it mean for you to believe in possibility?

Do you fall into thinking there is only one path to a dream? If so, how can you consider the many paths to make what you dream possible?

What would you do if you knew you could not fail?

CHAPTER 2

TRANSFORM FEAR INTO CURIOSITY

"I have no special talents. I am only passionately curious."
— *Albert Einstein*

There are points in my life where I look back and think that I was absolutely fearless. Moving to Boston, shortly after September 11, 2001, with no job, no apartment, and essentially no contacts was one of them. Perhaps in those moments my goals outweighed my fear, but ultimately, I still felt fearless.

Are there times in your life where you have felt fearless? How did that impact your life and the choices you made?

Somewhere along the way, I lost that fearlessness, and allowed fear to become a primary navigator in my life. The full realization of how much I was being guided by fear became clear to me a few years ago when I found myself in a time of crisis. I was miserable. In regard to my job, I dreaded going to work every day, feeling burnt out and unfulfilled. Yet I was afraid to make a change. My husband and I had just bought a house in the far too expensive Greater Boston area, and I was afraid that making a career move would compromise everything. How would we make ends meet if I took a lesser paying job? And to be honest, I was also afraid of falling on my face and being unsuccessful if I started my own business, which was really what I wanted to do. What if I let people down? People who'd thought I was successful and doing awesome work. I was afraid of trying something that might not work, and ultimately looking like a fool.

And so I stayed. And stayed. And stayed. I stayed for about five years longer than I should have, simply because I was afraid to do anything else.

Are there moments in your life when you have been driven by fear?

Believing in possibility is one thing, but the more you believe – especially in seemingly impossible things – the more fear is likely to join you on that journey. Often, some fear is a good thing. It's what keeps us safe in so many situations and has taught us about navigating life. Yet, for so many of us, instead of it being one of many tools and emotions that help guide and inform our lives, fear has taken a place in the driver's seat. It's shoved every other desire, emotion, and wealth of knowledge to the backseat. Well, let me tell you this: fear does not belong in the driver's seat, so if you are going to believe in possibility and pursue amazing possible and impossible things, then you are going to need to find a way to manage, and ultimately transform, that fear in a way that is useful in moving forward.

In my period of burnout and unfulfillment, I knew I'd reached a point where a change had to occur, and I needed to find a way to overcome my paralyzing fear that was keeping me stuck.

I am a naturally curious person – something I consider

one of my strongest qualities – and a friend gifted me with Brian Grazer's book, *A Curious Mind*. In reading this book, I was reminded of how curiosity can be used to transform fear. Curiosity is simply a desire to learn and to know. And so, instead of allowing myself to remain overwhelmed, stuck, or uncertain because of my fear, I started to ask questions and be inquisitive, both around what I was fearing and around the things I was dreaming and believing in.

The process of turning fear into curiosity is quite simple. Start by asking questions:

What can I learn from this?
What am I really afraid of?
What is the worst that can happen?

This last question can be a daunting question, but it's worth asking. In fear mode, we usually can jump to the worst-case scenario quickly, and feel as if it is going to be an immediate result. The important part of this question is to follow it up with what must occur between where you're at now, and the worst-case scenario occurring? Usually, there are significantly more steps involved than you might have imagined, and you don't have quite so much to fear as you thought.

As I started to reframe my fear into curiosity, something amazing happened. My fear started to shift. It never completely disappeared, and I don't think my fear ever will (or should). Instead, the energy surrounding my fear changed from being something that was causing me to feel stuck and stressed into being energy that excited me and invigorated me, inspiring me to learn and do more, and to create new ways of thinking about my situation.

Can you think of a time when you were experiencing the fight or flight response, in relation to a stressor that wasn't a life or death threat, and which you were able to channel the adrenaline into a productive response?

In the case of leaving my job and moving into something else, transforming fear into curiosity meant focusing on how I could learn more in order to make such a shift successful. How could I have authentic conversations with the important people in my life in order to share with them why I needed to make a change, and so that they could share in my journey more meaningfully? How could I prepare for mortgage payments and take steps to make a real change financially viable even if my job situation changed?

The purpose of starting simple, with questions, is not about knowing the right or perfect questions to ask. It's about the process of asking questions that will prompt learning, growth, and movement through the fear we're experiencing.

To transform fear into curiosity in your own life, I challenge you to take some time to define your fear. Sitting with our own fear is never a comfortable experience, but it is an informative one. How often are we afraid of something, but we can't explain where the sensation comes from? Or, we let a little, irrational fear take hold and dictate the decisions of our life as if it has become a matter of life and death. Take the time to really understand what you are fearing, and then start asking questions.

Ask questions that dig deep in understanding where your fear comes from and why it is a driver in your life. Follow your answers up with questions that start to transform the fear; ask questions that change your focus from what you are afraid of, to what you can learn from that fear. Then ask questions about where you want to be, what it will feel like when you are on the other side of your fear, and ultimately what you want to experience in the future.

Before you realize it, your questions will evolve past a focus on fear and where you're going, into questions about how to make the future you want possible, and an energy that will fuel the steps to come.

Ultimately, after a lot of preparatory work, I did make a leap from my full-time employment to living the life of a full-time entrepreneur. It wasn't easy, I admit. There were times when I wasn't sure how to make ends meet and times when I felt judged by others for not having it all figured out. I continued to revert to curiosity in the process – how could I learn from the challenges I was facing, and the growth opportunities that were before me. In the end, my new career path turned out to be more successful than I ever could have imagined — both in terms of the business, as well as the life I built for myself through the business.

And through it all, my biggest takeaway was this: Fear is best managed when you transform it into curiosity.

> *"Curiosity will conquer fear even more than bravery will."*
> *– James Stephens*

Questions for Reflection:

Is fear a driving factor in your life? If so, what are you so afraid of?

How can you be curious about the fear you are experiencing?

What questions can you ask about your current situations, and where you dream of going, that will help you transform your fear into curiosity?

CHAPTER 3

FAILURES ARE LESSONS. OBSTACLES ARE OPPORTUNITIES.

"Challenges are what makes life interesting. Overcoming them is what makes life meaningful." – Joshua J. Marine

If you are dreaming big dreams, if you are believing in possibility, and if you are putting yourself out there in the world, there is no doubt that you will experience obstacles and failures.

No matter what you are doing, failure and challenges are a fact of life. I shudder at almost every cliché about failures and obstacles, but I have to admit, there is much truth in them. Of course, as much as I know the value in obstacles and failure, I still prefer to avoid them at all costs. Don't we all?

Are there failures in your life that seemed to be without purpose? Or that you wish you could erase from your past? For me, and I would guess for you too, failures are the things that I most want to hide from others because I feel ashamed and embarrassed about my shortcomings. There is one story that I have especially resisted sharing with people for the last decade, because I was worried about how it would impact the ways in which others viewed me, but it's an applicable example for this chapter on failure and obstacles.

It was a few days before my birthday, I was celebrating my two-month wedding anniversary (yes, we were those people who celebrated every month), and it was the Friday afternoon starting off a long holiday weekend filled with fun plans with friends. A few minutes before 5pm, as I was preparing to walk out the door, my organization's vice president pulled me into a meeting room at the end of the hall. My heart was already aflutter with uncertainty as to the purpose of the meeting when she said, "Elizabeth, we don't think that you are performing to your potential here. It seems that it's time to part ways and let you go. If you can tell me here and now that your heart is here, that you're fully invested and committed to this job, and you're willing to give it more than 100% to grow, we can consider a trial period to keep you employed. But if not, this is your two weeks' notice."

Ouch. By the time she finished speaking, my heart was leaping out of my chest, my mind racing with the millions of thoughts and questions and fears (of course there were fears), wondering how to respond, where I would go from here. There was a part of me that wanted to attempt to save face and come up with all of the justifications as to why I hadn't been performing at the level expected, and promise that I'd dazzle the team in the coming weeks with my ability to turn it all around and excel at levels they'd seen when they first hired me. I knew I had that potential to excel. But those words weren't coming. Now, I can't even recall what I managed to say, although I did keep my composure long enough to collect my things from my desk and get into the elevator bank before completely losing it.

I was a failure. And I'd been fired.
My walk home was a blur as I wondered how I would tell

my husband. I panicked about what my friends would think. I questioned how I could possibly get another job with this red stain on my resume. And in the most "mature" mindset possible, I cancelled all plans for the weekend and spent a good amount of time moping about my failures and freaking out about how to make ends meet. Following that, I moved into an overdrive of activity as I tried to kick my butt into gear and update a resume I hadn't been expecting to need to rewrite, figuring out how to apply for unemployment, and re-doing budgets because our income had just been cut in half.

Responding in panic and urgency is not always the best way to recover from failures. And triaging obstacles is not usually the most productive way to overcome them. Usually they are short term solutions that are not well thought out and don't often take stock of the bigger picture. It also rushes us through the learning phase, because we are desperate to fix our situation, instead of looking to the root of the issue and addressing the challenge at its core.

While we don't always have the luxury of extended amounts of time to work through a failure or obstacle, they are best addressed when we can see the root of the failure or challenge and take time to reframe the situation.

After a few weeks of panic and unsuccessful attempts to jump into the first job that came my way, I was able to shift my thinking about what had occurred and reframe the situation.

Truth: I wasn't performing well at that job because my heart was no longer in it. At one point in time, the job had been an ideal fit for me, but I'd become bored, and I was ready to apply myself in new ways. While I'd still been performing at passable levels (or, I'd thought so, at least), it definitely wasn't living up to my potential or working with any sort of spark or passion.

Even when we can acknowledge these things ourselves, we certainly don't want others to see our weaknesses. I thought I was fooling everyone by staying in the job and going through the motions, but in fact I wasn't, and having my poor performance on display for everyone to see was a hard pill to swallow. But, also a necessary one.

This failure was an opportunity for me to learn – a LOT. I learned about myself as an employee… i.e., I'm not a very good employee if my heart isn't in it (true for a lot of us). I learned a lot about myself as a person… taking time to reflect on what lights me up, to learn new skills, to challenge myself in new ways. I learned about management and leadership… as much as that moment of being fired totally sucked, my VP handled it with an amazing amount of grace and compassion, which gave me the ability to walk out of that office with my dignity, despite the kick in the pants. And, I learned a lot about how I handle failure… i.e., jumping right into immediate solutions and redirection, which I've since learned to temper with time so that I'm more able to reflect, and learn, and reframe.

You might be asking, what exactly does it mean to reframe a failure? This goes hand in hand with the curiosity that comes with transforming fear. Reframing means to look at, present, or think of beliefs, ideas, and situations in a new or different way, and to change the focus or perspective.

I always start this process, be it with a failure or an obstacle I'm facing, with the question: *What can I learn from this?* This is never meant to mitigate the hard situation you might be presented with, but instead it should help you broaden your perspective of the experience.

The next question I usually ask is: *Are there any unforeseen benefits that I haven't yet recognized?* In the case of being fired, one unforeseen benefit was the ability to reevaluate what I wanted to do with my career, and focus my job search on roles that I would find more fulfilling. While I would have preferred to do that on my own time and in my own way, this was something positive I could try to take away from the experience. A dear friend's mother was recently diagnosed with cancer and is in chemotherapy at the moment. In the midst of this incredibly difficult situation, my friend has seen her relationship with her mom grow stronger as a result of the time she is spending to help her mom navigate treatments. I'm not saying that the benefit will make everything worthwhile, but even in the darkest moments I am always looking for some glimmer of light, something good that can come as a result.

When I struggle to reframe a failure or obstacle, I realize that I'm often too close to the situation to be able to see it through a different lens. When we are in the midst of hardship, often we have tunnel vision as we struggle to move through the difficulty. In these times, I ask those closest to me to help me see things from a different perspective. Are there lessons or benefits they acknowledge that I'm not seeing myself? What are they observing from their outside perspective?

Finding my next job was an uphill battle, and a far more difficult challenge than what I had anticipated. My job search ended up taking ten months in total. Ten long, arduous months. Ten months of learning what failure looked like up close and personal. Ten months of gleaning every lesson possible from that failure, so that I could reframe it as a learning opportunity instead of it being simply a red mark on my resume. Ten months of obstacles that I slowly learned to reframe as opportunities for refining what was most important to me.

Reframing is not a one-time shift of perspective. It is an ongoing process that builds upon the questions asked and lessons learned in the prior moment, to continue evolving.

Those ten months between when I was fired and when I found a new job became opportunities for me to learn new skills and enhance my resume, opportunities to volunteer and give back to my community, and opportunities to work in many different offices as a temp and meet a lot of new people.

In that season it was not always easy to see my failure as a lesson or to see the challenges and obstacles I faced as opportunities. But I can see now that it wasn't until I was able to reframe my failures and obstacles that I was able to move forward.

"I have not failed. I've just found 10,000 ways that won't work. Many of life's failures are people who did not realize how close they were to success when they gave up." – Thomas Edison

I love this Thomas Edison quote because it is the ultimate example of reframing failure, and a reminder of why not to give up when we are faced with failure and challenges. After even 1,000 attempts that failed, I probably would have been ready to give up and move on to something else, but Edison saw it all as part of learning and embraced the process. Perhaps this is the most important key of reframing failure and challenges – by learning to embrace the process.

Failure is not fun. It's hard and messy and embarrassing a lot of the time. But it's also imperative to our growth, to our lives. The ability to learn from our failures, and see inevitable obstacles as opportunities, is critical to an optimistic life. Instead of being things that define us for what we are not able to overcome, failure and obstacles becomes a stepping stones to our future of possibility.

Questions for Reflection:

What failures and obstacles are you letting define you?

How can you reframe these failures as lessons?

Are there obstacles and challenges that you are facing now which seem insurmountable?

What opportunities are in these challenges that you haven't yet allowed yourself to recognize?

Are you too close to your situation to be able to look at it through a different lens? If so, who can you ask to help you view things from a different perspective?

CHAPTER 4

BE ROOTED IN BELIEF

"A man lives by believing something."
– Thomas Carlyle

An optimistic mindset is rooted deeply in belief. Believing in possibility, as we've already explored, is one of these key beliefs. Believing in possibility is what moves you forward and gives you branches that reach for the sky. Similarly, you need beliefs that ground you. When fear and failure and obstacles are present, you need to know what you believe – at your core. You need to know where your foundation lies in order to keep believing in possibility, and to, ultimately, take action that moves you towards the possibility you seek.

Do you know what foundations ground you when life feels in chaos? Are there truths that you constantly come back to as a guiding force for your life?

For me, I've found that foundation lies in three key belief structures. While I believe these are universal, and adaptable to each individual, it is less important that you believe these three things specifically and more important that you know what you believe.

Belief In Yourself

"Once we believe in ourselves, we can risk curiosity, wonder, spontaneous delight, or any experience that reveals the human spirit." – E.E. Cummings

Ultimately, unless we believe in ourselves, it is virtually impossible to hold space for optimism in our own hearts and lives. Believing in ourselves is the launching point we need for taking on a mindset of optimism and turning it into a life of optimistic action. This is where the rubber hits the road with our doubt-defying state of mind.

You might be thinking, this is all well and good, but I'm not sure – deep down – that I believe in myself. What does that really mean? And how do I even do it?

In it's simplest form, believing in yourself is about:
(1) knowing and appreciating who you are, your unique traits, your strengths, and your weaknesses
(2) trusting yourself
(3) believing that you are worthy of your dreams and goals

This doesn't mean that you will never have self-doubt, or that you'll never question who you are or what you want or even what you deserve, but it means – in the grand scheme of things – that you are in touch with yourself, with who you are and who you want to become, and that you believe in your potential. Believing in yourself gives you the foundation that you need to believe in possibility, the belief that fear can be transformed, and the belief that you can overcome failure and obstacles. It gives you a drive, and confidence, to keep moving forward.

Belief In A Higher Power

"I believe in Christianity as I believe that the Sun has risen not only because I see it but because by it I see everything else."
– C.S. Lewis

For me, belief in a higher power means believing in God. For you, this might be the Universe, or Mother Nature.

I grew up in a Christian home, raised by Christian parents and as part of a Christian community, which has informed my faith and my beliefs throughout my entire life. While my belief in God, and in Jesus Christ, has been unwavering for as long as I can remember, the application of that faith has been anything but traditional, and it continues to evolve as I grow and mature. There have been seasons of my life where I have spent every Sunday worshipping in church, every Wednesday night in a church Bible Study or community group, and praying and reading my Bible every day while serving my church community throughout the week. Then there have been other seasons of my life where months or years have passed between church visits, and when I couldn't have told you the last time I read my Bible or prayed, because I was angry with God or uncertain about the application of my faith at that time.

Regardless of the season of my life, or the intensity of the application of my faith, my faith in God has always been a constant. I, like C.S. Lewis, believe that my belief is what lights the way for everything else. It is my foundation from which I am constantly learning and growing and seeking. My belief is at the heart of who I am: it defines me, and it equips me for hope and optimism.

Whether it is through God as I view God, the god of your own faith, or some other higher power, I encourage you to believe in something greater than yourself. Something which lights the way for you to see everything else.

Belief In Wonder

"We need a renaissance of wonder. We need to renew, in our hearts and in our souls, the deathless dream, the eternal poetry, the perennial sense that life is miracle and magic."
— E. Merrill Root

Wonder can take on many forms. As Root eludes to in this quote, wonder can be miracles or magic, wonder can be an awe at the world and of the universe, wonder can be appreciation for art and life.

Many people consider me to be a very serious person, often too serious, but people who know me well know that my life is tinged with a lot of whimsy. As much as I have a grounded belief in God, I also believe in magic. Sometimes that's in the form of miracles that are most certainly coming from God, sometimes it's winks from the universe, and sometimes it's just serendipity. I still wish on shooting stars and birthday candles, I believe in fairy-tales, and I think there is inexplicable magic in connection and kisses and travel.

What gives you a sense of wonder in your life? Do you believe in magic or winks from the universe? Do you make wishes or acknowledge miracles?

There is much in this world that cannot be explained or

defined, and it is these things that can give us wonder. This sense of magic, of wonder, is what helps us not take life too seriously, and at the same time, keep exploring and moving forward with whimsy and curiosity. It is part of what allows us to dream, to believe in possibility, to reach for the stars, and to fall in love. It drives us to search for wisdom, to explore the unknown, to strive for bigger and better things. I believe that we all need to believe in magic and wonder to appreciate the unexplainable things in life.

Do these beliefs resonate with you, in a way that you can adapt them to what you believe and how you see the world? If not, I encourage you to take some time to explore what beliefs you feel grounded in, and how they give you a foundation for the life you want to live.

Questions for Reflection:

What does it mean for you to believe in yourself?

What does belief in a higher power look like for you?

What is the foundation that gives you room to believe in bigger and better things, to reach for the stars?

PART 2

PRACTICAL OPTIMISM

Now that we've touched on the foundations for an optimistic mindset, it's time to move into the practical aspects. How do you practice optimism? This section includes my tangible tips and tools for making your optimism an integral, active, practical part of your everyday life. I've broken this down into 4 key categories: work, relationships, community, and self. Within each topic, I've included 2-3 practical applications for you to use in your own life.

As you explore each of these components, I encourage you to adapt the suggestions to your own life however you see fit. While these are tried and true tips for living a life of practical optimism, this section is by no means exhaustive. What worked for me might not work exactly the same for you. Learn what you can, use what you can, and create your own tools for applying optimism to your life.

Ultimately, practical optimism will lead to more inspired living.

THE OPTIMIST'S MANIFESTO

PART 2: SECTION 1

OPTIMISM & WORK

Of our four categories involved in discussing practical optimism, work seems like the natural place to start. On average, people spend a third of their life working – which is a larger proportion of time than what's given to most any other aspect of life (even sleeping) – so it makes sense that work has a significant impact on our life and on our outlook on life.

At the individual level, optimism is important to work because studies have shown that people who are optimistic have more satisfaction in their jobs, and more success in job-hunting and promotions. With the amount of time spent at work, our satisfaction and success carries over into our general satisfaction and viewpoint on life.

As organizations, optimism is important because it builds stronger teams, increases employee engagement, and develops a more positive workplace culture. Organizations that have cultures of optimism tend to be more progressive, experience higher customer engagement, and be more profitable.

Optimism at work encompasses all of the categories with which we will discuss practical optimism, since within our work we are also existing within a community, in relationship with other people, and yet remaining distinct as an individual. The practical optimism outlined here, more so than in any other category, is transferrable and applicable to every part of our lives.

CHAPTER 5
LIVE FOR A CAUSE,
NOT FOR APPLAUSE

"Have the courage to follow your heart and intuition.
They somehow already know what you truly want to become.
Everything else is secondary." – Steve Jobs

Optimism in your work is rooted in knowing why you are doing what you are doing, in being rooted in a purpose and a cause, rather than trying to please others or for the accolades and outside opinions of what your life, and your work, should look like. People like Steve Jobs are a great example of optimism in work. An optimist himself, he has been quoted countless times for telling people to find a passion and follow a why.

I have never been one of those people who always knew what I wanted to be when I grew up, whose life was spent planning for one career and a linear career path. My path has been quirky and circuitous and anything but clear. But one thing has been apparent throughout the entire process – when I'm pursuing something I'm passionate about, I am much more successful than when I do something because someone else wants me to do it, or because it's something that looks good on my resume.

Do you know what you are most passionate about? Does

that passion translate to your work?

Finding what you are most passionate about, and how it relates and translates to work, can be a long process because it isn't always apparent based solely on the ways in which we excel.

My first real job was as a high school intern in the finance department of Hewlett Packard. I have a knack for numbers, and math and accounting come easily to me. I recall the project I was assigned at the beginning of my first summer interning; it was a financial analysis project that was expected to take me the duration of the summer. Three weeks later, I had completed the project and I was thirsting for more. That project set the stage for me quickly establishing myself as a great candidate for employment and gave me a lot of encouragement to pursue a career in finance, with the promise of a full-time job at HP upon graduation. I spent my senior year of high school through my sophomore year of college as a part of the finance department at HP, and everyone thought that I was set. I was destined to use that launching pad to become the CEO of a Fortune 500 company – a dream that was much more my father's than my own, but which seemed enticing none the less.

As would be the case with the job I'd get fired from later on in life, my heart was not in finance or accounting, despite my natural tendencies. The idea of consulting excited me, and I wanted to engage with people on a more personal level, to explore hospitality, to write and travel, and eventually start my own company. Working in the finance department of a prominent tech company didn't light my fire, no matter how great a trajectory it might offer. So, despite the accolades, and the promise for full-time employment upon graduation, I only got about halfway through college before I decided to blaze a different trail and pursue entrepreneurship and event planning.

How do you put your heart into your work? What drives you? When do you find the most pride in your work?

In living, and working, for a cause, I have found the following steps are a great place to start.

Define Your Purpose

"The purpose of life is a life of purpose." – Robert Bryne

Take some time to reflect upon your purpose. Why do you get up every day? Are you doing a specific type of work to please others? Are you doing it because you are good at it? Are you doing it because it's the way you can make an income and make ends meet? What is your purpose in working?

Sometimes our purpose, what drives us, is about providing for our family – that's our cause, regardless of the actual work we do. Other times we are driven because we have an innovation that we want to bring to the world, and we will stop at nothing to do so. Our purpose can be a social condition we want to change and impact, or a passion and talent we have for numbers, the options are limitless.

There are no rules for what your purpose should be, but it is critical for you to know what it is so that it can inform your mindset and your choices on the days when you're finding it hard to wake up at 5 a.m. for the work that needs to be finished, or when you have to skip dinner with your family. It's also important to know your purpose for those times when you fail, and inevitably you will, because the cause you are living for is the reason you'll get up and start all over again the next day.

Embrace Your Passions

"Passion is energy. Feel the power that comes from focusing on what excites you." – Oprah Winfrey

Never discount the value of what lights you up, what gives you a spark and energy. The things that we are passionate about are often the things we will be most successful in – because they are the things we are willing to work hard and long towards, they are the things that we talk about to no end, the things that we would likely do for free.

The source of the light in us can come from a variety of different places. I have found that it often comes from the people I work with and the excitement I feel in collaborating with others towards a shared mission, rather than in the exact work that I am doing. A light can come from the impact that we are making to change something, or the freedom a job gives us to travel the world.

Sometimes our purpose and our passions are the same things, but they can also be independent as well, so take the time to keep digging and to seek out the role that your purpose and passion each play in your life and your work.

Make A Difference

"The ones who are crazy enough to think that they can change the world, are the ones who do." – Steve Jobs

No one has the same combination of gifts and talents and placement in this world as you. So, you can – and should – make a unique contribution that makes a difference to those around you and to this world. Your cause, what you work towards, can impact others in countless ways if you allow it to do so. While we often think of making a difference as something that happens on a large scale, all it takes is a single act of kindness to make a difference. From the way you interact with colleagues and clients, the pride you take in your work product, mentoring others in your profession to grow, or using your professional skills to volunteer in your community, you can always make a difference.

A significant component of working for a cause is knowing how what you do is bigger than yourself, and knowing that it can and will make a difference.

Questions for Reflection:

Are you living for a cause? If so, what is it?

Do you know what your purpose is in life and in work?

What is your passion?

How are you making a difference through your work?

CHAPTER 6

COLLABORATE, DON'T COMPETE

"Competition makes us faster. Collaboration makes us better."
– Unknown

There's an old proverb: "A rising tide lifts all boats." This is the epitome of collaboration – we are all working together for a greater result in the end. Open-source software is a great example of collaboration. Developers engaging in open-sourcing make their code available for free and encourage improvements and modifications. This is a way of sharing the best practices and expertise while also asking for help, and it creates new, improved codes that go beyond what anyone could master or develop on their own.

How have you collaborated with others in your work?

For almost 10 years, I was with a high-end event planning company in Boston, first as an individual contributor and then as the managing director. The firm, as directed by the owner, was fiercely competitive with everything about their business. From relations with competitive companies in the area on to the level with which they'd provide information to their clients, to ideas which were considered intellectual property, the culture of the organization was one of competition and guardedness instead of one of collaboration.

Eventually, I started my own business in a similar arena. As someone who does not have a competitive spirit for the most part, I sought to approach my business from a culture of collaboration – collaborating with my clients in a way that set us up as a bigger part of the same team, working together with other event planners who were often considered competitors in my industry, and collaborating with the sharing of ideas and best practices to improve our industry and businesses as a whole. What I found in response was a delightful surprise at the way in which my business blossomed because of such collaboration, and before I knew it, my business was more successful than I ever could have dreamed. What was even better was the quality of connection and engagement between myself and everyone I worked with – my clients, my vendors, my competitors, and my team. With a culture of collaboration, we treated each other with more trust, deeper respect for contributions, and support through problem-solving, and as a result, we had a greater impact on our industry and the businesses involved at every level. The events we produced superseded anything I had accomplished previously because I was now gleaning knowledge from everyone's unique experience in order to create a result that was even better than any of us could have imagined… because we weren't doing it alone.

What would it look like if you collaborated with colleagues, clients, and even competitors?

Collaboration is important to optimism in the workplace because it enables us to work towards the best possible outcomes. It creates more positive working environments when we work together with, instead of against, others. We benefit by broadening our perspectives and skill sets in order to create the best end product. Collaboration, and the resulting successes, create a sense of pride and inclusiveness among our teams, and for us as individuals.

So, how do we successfully collaborate, instead of compete?

Show Up

"Eighty percent of success is showing up." – Woody Allen

Collaboration is successful when we all show up as the best versions of ourselves, and authentically share the expertise, best practices, and unique perspectives that we have. No one will ever be able to identically replicate who we are or how we do something, so we need to relinquish the fear of being "copied" or having our ideas "stolen". Instead, we need to openly share so that we can not only help others grow and improve, but continue to further refine, adapt, and improve our own contributions.

How can you show up more in your work? Is there a committee you can volunteer to be a part of, or a new employee that you can offer to mentor? Or, is there expertise that only you have, that you can offer to share with others?

Ask For Help

"We don't build trust when we offer help. We build trust when we ask for it." – Simon Sinek

In addition to collaboration coming from sharing our own best practices and expertise, collaboration exists best when we can admit what we don't know and ask for help. Recognizing that others have different experiences, expertise, and talents, and then listening and learning, enables us to grow and expand on our own thinking and understanding. As Sinek points out above, asking for help is also a way in which we build trust, a key component of collaborating successfully with others. In the vulnerability it exhibits, asking for help creates an environment where everyone feels comfortable asking for help. The dialogue and problem-solving that occurs in response takes the collaboration to a new level of interaction and results.

In what ways can you ask for help from others? Is there something you'd really like to learn at work, that you can pursue in order to grow and contribute more?

Give Praise

"It is amazing what you can accomplish when you do not care who gets the credit." – Harry S. Truman

Recognizing the contributions of others is critical to forming a culture of collaboration instead of competition. When we are greedy with receiving credit, we foster competition, distrust, and a lack of sharing. On the other hand, when we are generous with sharing credit and recognition for accomplishments, everyone benefits. Be generous in sharing praise with others, and in recognizing individual contributions and strengths. Acknowledge the team effort that was required for the accomplishments at hand.

What have you been working on recently? How can you recognize the efforts of those around you?

Questions for Reflection:

In what areas of your work are you collaborating with others?

In what areas of your work are you competing? Are there ways to shift that to collaboration?

CHAPTER 7

INSPIRE SOLUTIONS

"If your actions inspire others to dream more, learn more, do more, and become more, you are a leader." – John Quincy Adams

Optimism in the workplace is not only about your own mindset in the work you are doing, but serving as inspiration for yourself, and for others.

Who in your life has been a source of inspiration for you? Is there someone who helps you see solutions, and create solutions in your life?

During my junior year of college at Pepperdine University, I worked with a start-up founded by recent Pepperdine grads. Our motley crew consisted of three surfers from Orange County, with respective degrees from the business, communications and biology departments, and myself, a business major and girl-next-door type from Idaho. Over the summer we took a road trip to Silicon Valley to meet with potential angel investors and spent three days sharing our story, presenting our ideas, and attempting to garner support for the business.

On the last night of our trip, we were invited to a cocktail party with some of the A-list investors we had met during our visit. The invitation encouraged "festive" attire suiting an art gallery soiree. After living mostly out of the car between meetings, and with all of us crashing in a cozy, shared hotel room, our "festive" attire options were a little worse for the wear, but we dressed up as best we could and made our way to downtown San Francisco. One of my surfer colleagues was dressed in jeans and a flamboyant silk jacket comprised of Picasso mosaics, and the other two guys had donned suits straight from the 70s (slightly out of place in 2000), complete with blue and yellow ruffled shirts and full on polyester, and I was sporting a black dress with embroidered oriental designs (not your typical black dress, but rather tame compared to the rest of my team). Our grand entrance to the cocktail party could have made records screech to a stop as we walked into a room filled with dark suits. As we learned later, from the host, his request for "festive" attire had been intended as encouragement to his investment colleagues to lighten up a little and perhaps don a festive tie or go tieless. He'd never expected a festive interpretation from four college students.

About 45 minutes into the party, as we mingled and introduced ourselves to the investment community in attendance, a familiar question started to be posed. "What made you decide to crash this party? How'd you get in?" As amusing as the questions were, it was equally entertaining to watch each questioner's reaction as we shared that we were on the guest list, invited by the host himself, one of the top angel investors in the Valley. Once the host had gotten a kick out of everyone's impressions as well, we started playing with the perceptions and concocting stories of how, and why, we had "crashed" the party.

Throughout our entire Silicon Valley trip, from the formal meetings to the "festive" cocktail party, whether the people we met chose to invest in the company or not, one thing remained consistent – everyone kept encouraging our vision and inspiring solutions, for the company as a whole, for the next steps in our business model and financing, and for us as individuals. Everyone we met with not only saw potential in what we were currently doing, but also in what we might do in the future, and so we had an amazing wealth of wisdom, insight, advice, new connections, and financial support to catapult us to the next level of innovation and growth. Those three days with the team of investors taught me more about inspiring others than would have been the case if they had simply signed over a check and underwritten the company, which no one did. Instead, they inspired the four of us to dream bigger, to dig deeper, and to broaden our idea of solutions.

While my time at that start-up was relatively short-lived, the lessons from that time have stayed with me. Over my 22+ years in all facets of business, I have found the following to be key components to inspiring solutions.

Be A Voice, Not An Echo

"A man's mind, stretched by a new idea, can never go back to its original dimensions." – Oliver Wendall Holmes

Inspiring solutions is about helping people see what could be, not simply what is. Share your original thoughts and ideas, your visions, your dreams, your version of what is possible. In doing this, instead of echoing only what you've heard, you allow others to share their original thoughts and ideas as well.

It's about thinking bigger, thinking outside of the box, and even about not believing that a box exists for a given discussion. It's about giving yourself, and others, the permission to dream, to brainstorm with no restrictions. It's about having space to question, to experiment, and to explore.

Foster Conversation And Open Dialogue

"A real conversation always contains an invitation. You are inviting another person to reveal herself or himself to you, to tell you who they are or what they want." – David Whyte

Fostering conversation and creating a space, and opportunity, for open dialogue is critical to inspiring solutions. When colleagues, employees, managers, and anyone else for that matter, feel that they are invited to speak their mind, to share their vision and idea, then new visions and ideas and solutions are formed. Our workplaces have grown stagnant in many ways because it is easier to remain quiet than to suggest an idea that might not work, or an idea that requires a lot more work to explore, or an idea that just hasn't been vetted yet. Instead, we need to be encouraging these conversations which spark others to think differently, to share their unique insights and expertise, and to suggest solutions to problems we didn't even know existed. This is when the stagnation in the workplace will cease and we will be overcome with inspiration, innovation, solutions and growth.

Give Space For Failure

"I can accept failure, everyone fails at something. But I can't accept not trying." – Michael Jordan

As we've covered already, failure is inevitable. Learning to deal with our own failure is one thing, but fostering it as a normal course of life, and of work, is another. In order to inspire solutions, one must give space for others to fail as a part of innovation and exploration. As much as we try to transform fear into curiosity, and learn from our failures, giving space for others to do the same is critical to creating workplaces that actually inspire innovation. Part of giving space for such failure means sharing our failure with others as well, both to help others learn from our example and to show that failure is acceptable, that it isn't permanent. Create an environment which celebrates failure as part of the process, and more solutions will be inspired as a result.

Questions for Reflection:

How can you inspire solutions today?

How can you create conversations of inspiration?

Do you give space for others to fail? Do you celebrate the process of failure for yourself and others?

PART 2: SECTION 2

OPTIMISM & RELATIONSHIPS

There is very little in our lives that doesn't involve relationships, whether it's a relationship with your boss or a colleague at work, your relationship with those closest to you such as your spouse or kids or friends, or a relationship with the cashier at your corner store or in the community you've built at church or volunteering at a local non-profit. Notably, there is also a lot of crossover between relationships in every aspect of our lives, so I've sandwiched the relationships section between work and community – knowing that these components of optimism & relationships relate to both, as well as standing on their own.

For most of us, relationships have the most significant impact on our state of being. When we have healthy, fulfilling, and meaningful relationships with others, it has a positive influence on our overall mindset, health, and happiness.

Optimism is critical in relationships because it is what allows us to look for the best in others, and work towards better and more fulfilling connection with the people in our lives. Studies have proven that optimists also have longer, more satisfying, and happier relationships.

In this next section you will learn tips to apply optimism in your relationships, in order to build more connection, fulfillment, satisfaction, and happiness with the people you are in relationship with in every aspect of your life.

CHAPTER 8

MAGNIFY STRENGTHS

"We rise by lifting others." – Robert Ingersoll

Today's society seems to love illuminating the weaknesses of others. Just peruse YouTube or the news and you will find plenty of videos and stories of someone's failure or mishap. What would it look like though if we set others up for success, instead of failure? If we illuminated their strengths, instead of their weaknesses? How does it feel for you if those around you downplay your weaknesses, and instead highlight the strengths that make you shine?

One of the most influential moments for me was when a relatively new friend of mine went out of her way to help highlight my strengths and help me to shine, and it completely shifted how I want to support others. When I decided to leave my full time job as a director of operations for one of the leading event planning companies in Boston, in order to start my own business, many people thought I was crazy. Why would I leave something that seemed like a certainty for something that involved a lot of risk?

My friend, Diana, was a full-time director of events for a venue in Boston, and had a great resume of planning events both in that role and in her prior position as a planner for a nationally known celebrity event planner. In terms of my event planning career, she was who I aspired to be. Diana was the first person who called me out on living a life behind the scenes, in place of stepping into my own abilities to shine. She encouraged me to use my strengths to serve others on a larger scale where I could make a significant difference in my industry and my community. Once I had made the decision to go out on my own, Diana was there at every step, helping me to review and refine my proposals. She was sending me potential gigs at each and every turn, and she was offering her help and support wherever possible along the way.

This was the start of a beautiful friendship as they say, or rather, a beautiful partnership. Diana and I began to collaborate together on a number of projects – sometimes under the umbrella of my business, and sometimes under the umbrella of hers. Between the two of us, we built a relationship around magnifying each other's strengths – where my strengths lie in client relations, fundraising, and catering, other aspects such as AV and stage management are not my strong suit, whereas Diana excels at directing a show, managing the lighting and sound components, and executing large scale logistics. Our partnership offered the ideal opportunity for each of us to shine where we were strongest, and rely on the other person to shine where we were weak. It is a true collaboration that has made us both excel, individually and in the way in which we connect and relate to each other.

This example is one of those that traverses areas of work, relationships, and personal life. Magnifying strengths plays a key role in building more satisfying and fulfilling relationships, and deeper connection with those around you.

Are there people in your life that you spend time focusing on weaknesses, instead of strengths? Or relationships that seem to focus more on criticism, instead of building each other up? What would it look like for you to magnify the strengths of those around you?

Here are the most useful ways I've found to magnify strengths in the relationships in my life, leading to more meaningful connection in those relationships.

Compliment

One of the non-profit clients I work with has a teenage client whose mission is to change the world one compliment at a time. She is one of those individuals of whom I am constantly in awe, and I'm humbled by her wisdom, wit, and view on the world.

Complimenting people is one of the best, and easiest, ways to start magnifying their strengths. Whether it is in the form of a compliment to the person directly, or praise to a boss, a client, or an observer, acknowledging other's strengths is a sure way to start magnifying them.

When we compliment another person, it is a way to not only acknowledge their unique and wonderful gifts, but also reflect them back in recognition and praise. It is a way to tell another person "I see you," and "I appreciate who you are and what you have to offer."

Create Opportunities To Shine

Simply acknowledging strengths is not enough; we must give others a space to shine. As I mentioned at the beginning of the chapter, too often, as a society, we find pleasure in setting people up for failure. Asking a question we know someone doesn't have the right answer to, or creating a situation where their weaknesses will be exposed and somehow we are proved right, or superior. This is not the right environment in which to foster optimism or to magnify strengths. Instead, we need to create opportunities for individuals' strengths to be utilized and put on display.

In the case of Diana and me, we created a partnership in which each of us focused on our areas of expertise and strength, and we relied on the other person to focus on their strengths which also happened to be an area of weakness or a growth opportunity for the other one of us. In this case, it was a win-win; not only was my own strength magnified, but in the process, I created opportunities to magnify another's strengths, as well.

How would you feel if you were set up for success, if others in your life gave opportunities for your strengths to be on full display? Now, how can you do that for others?

Play A Supporting Role

Sometimes magnifying another's strengths means playing a supporting role. Whether this is accomplished through helping to orchestrate from behind the scenes, when no one will ever know your involvement, or playing a pivotal role on stage where you are creating the foundation for another person to look and perform at their best, supporting roles are what help define us as individuals and define others' strengths.

For Diana and me, ego (thankfully) did not play a part in our partnerships – when it was her time to shine, I was more than happy to hand out her business card and praise her at every turn – and vice versa. Yet, I never could have taken the leading role without a strong person to support me and help me to succeed. Someone who knew my strengths, even when, at times, I questioned them myself, and someone who helped me succeed.

Along the same lines as providing an opportunity for others to shine, in what way can you play a supporting role for another person? Is there a newer employee at your company that you can offer support to in order to help them grow? Do you have a friend that wants to try a new skill, and can you support her in that endeavor? Does your spouse or partner have an opportunity to step up into a leadership role at work or in the community, and in what way can you support that next step?

While magnifying strengths is often about others, specifically as it relates to our relationships and setting our ego aside to help others, I would be remiss here if I didn't take a moment to focus on the role that magnifying strengths plays in relation to ourselves as well. As important as it is in our relationships with others, Simon Sinek beautifully acknowledges that "Focusing on our own strengths is what, in fact, makes us strong." In the same way that we must believe in ourselves, there is a place, an importance, to recognizing and magnifying our own strengths. To knowing when we should step forward and claim our strengths, and when we need to rely on others to support us in our weakness.

Questions for Reflection:

What would it look like if you magnified the strengths of others, instead of focusing on their shortcomings?

Whose strengths can you magnify today? Someone at work? Your spouse? Your kids?

Are there strengths – your own, or someone else's – that you are overlooking?

How can you bring those strengths into the limelight?

CHAPTER 9

SEE THE LIGHT IN OTHERS

" Help others see their potential so they are inspired to achieve it."
– Adriaan Groenewald

W hat you focus on expands. This is one of those truths that is easily overlooked, but applies to almost every aspect of life. If we focus on the good, there is more good to see. If we focus on the bad, it seems like that is all there is. The same is true for what we focus on in others. By focusing on the good, the light, of those around you, you help to bring out the best in them. You reinforce it. You help it grow, expand, and take root. When the best parts of ourselves are recognized, we want to continue showing up with those best parts. And when the good in us is celebrated, we want to live up to the good that is seen in us.

This seems to be easy early on in relationships. At this stage, there's newness, excitement, and learning. It's easy for "love to be blind" as they say, and to overlook the less desirable traits in someone, to give a lot of grace to their shortcomings, and see only their potential. As time goes on, we often lose sight of the light in others as we get caught up in the day to day, and suddenly we are experiencing people in their fullness – which includes both positive and negative characteristic traits, for all of us. And without meaning to, we often start to focus more on the dark than on the light.

My husband and I have been married for 13 years now, and when I was young and naïve and in love, I thought that our marriage – at least in so far as we relate to each other – would never have difficulty or struggle. Funny, right? I knew we'd have challenges that we'd have to deal with as they related to job and family, but certainly not with each other.

A few years ago, though, our marriage reached a breaking point. We were so busy with our lives – both of us owners of our own businesses, managing a rental property, immersing ourselves in errands and activities, and juggling volunteer commitments and community involvement – I think we stopped seeing each other. Not only were we not seeing the light in each other, we just weren't seeing each other at all. We were ships passing in the night, seemingly moving in very different directions. When we did see each other, it was logistical – *Is the apartment rented? Here's my travel schedule for work. When are we doing that project for the church?* – And when it wasn't logistical, it was often focused on our shortcomings – *I'm disappointed that you didn't plan a date night. I'm angry that you won't look up from your phone when we're having a conversation. I'm sad that we aren't connecting, and this isn't working.* From the outside, many people didn't understand – it seemed like we had the perfect marriage. But isn't that always the case? Looking in from the outside never offers an accurate reflection of what is happening on the inside.

Are there relationships like this in your life? Whether with a spouse, a friend, a sibling, or a co-worker? Someone with whom you connected great with early on, you saw amazing parts of them, and yet now, years later, that shine is wearing off? Which relationships in your life are on autopilot, going about routine, but lacking that deeper connection?

What would it look like for you to return to the early days of those relationships, the time of deeper connection when it was easier to see the good in the other person? How would it feel for you, instead of being caught in the day-to-day, to feel like you are being seen for the light that shines from deep within?

As for my husband and me, we tried countless things to work on our marriage. Counseling? Check. More time together, in the form of date nights and trips? Check. Time apart? Check. Support and advice from friends? Check. Reading marriage books? Check. You name it, we were trying it, or willing to try it. Did some of these things help? Yes, on occasion, or for a short period of time, but rarely were the impacts lasting. For a significant period of time, we just continued to find ourselves right back in the same place.

My husband's 40th birthday was coming up, and I was going to be away on an extended trip, missing his birthday. As I reflected on what to do to celebrate him, and his 40 years, I started to think about his light – his unique personality, and gifts, skills, talents, and humor – all of the things I'd appreciated in countless ways when we'd first been dating, but didn't spend the time taking note of the same way as I once had. So, for his birthday, I put together a celebration of 40 things that were his unique light, that I loved and embraced and wanted to celebrate. In doing so, I spent much more time focusing on the things that are great about my husband, in place of focusing on all of the things that weren't working in our marriage.

This one act didn't dramatically change things overnight, but it changed my perspective. It reminded me of where I want to focus, and also of the benefits of focusing on the light in others. My husband responded to that celebration of light, and sparks in him that I hadn't witnessed in years started to make themselves known again. When I commented on his humor, something that made me first fall in love with him, he shared that side of himself more and we found inside jokes once again. In celebrating our shared passion for food and wine and cooking together, he started to suggest more ideas for meals to cook in collaboration. And as I repeated this process of finding more ways to see the light in him, he shone better and brighter than before. As a result, he started to see the light in me again, in new and different ways.

I'm sure by now you're thinking "That's all well and good, but this doesn't sound very practical or tangible; it just sounds like a mindset shift." In many ways it is about mindset and perspective, but what is more important are the actions you take as a result of your mindset and perspective. Here are some of the practical actions that I recommend.

Treat Them As If Their Light Is All You See

"See the light in others, and treat them as if that's all you see."
– Dr. Wayne Dyer

Everyone is a sum of all of their parts, but too often we treat people as if they are defined by their shortcomings, or mistakes, instead of seeing the entire person. On the contrary, I propose that we take Dr. Dyer's advice and treat people as if they are defined only by the light in them, by their potential, by the good they bring. So often, we are our own harshest critics, and no one is benefited if the people in our lives are also harsh critics of us. I'm not saying that we don't accept the people in our lives in their entirety, flaws and all, but we can treat them as if they are always the best version of themselves – with the same grace and acceptance as we do when we first fell in love with them.

Instead of complaining or criticizing, which comes so easily to many of us, shift your focus to the positive. Highlighting strengths, praising, and complimenting are all ways to bring out the positive traits of those around us. I challenge you to start with trying just 1 day without complaining about or criticizing another person. Replace those comments with celebrating the unique, light-filled traits that you cherish and admire, and see what unfolds. Then, try it for 1 week, and then for 1 month. It's beautiful to see another person's light shine bigger and brighter as that light is regularly recognized and celebrated.

Always Assume Positive Intent

"I always prefer to believe the best about everybody, it saves so much trouble." – Richard Kipling

In our culture of pessimism, we seem to have also become a culture of cynics – always waiting for the other shoe to drop. This has evolved into assuming the worst case scenarios, not only in the big picture of our lives, but also in our relationships. We take something relatively minor – someone forgets to call on our birthday, or misses a date we had scheduled – and blow it out of proportion in a negative way, assuming it means that they don't love us, that something tragic has happened to them, or that they've found someone else. Instead, what's most often the case is that their life got busy, or they got caught up at work, or their kids were sick, or any number of mundane things happened, to where life simply got in the way. In a case like this, the one minor thing which upset us really has little bearing on the foundation of feelings in a relationship or the value of a relationship, yet we take so many things to the extreme that that's forgotten.

Assuming positive intent, in every case, seems to be much less trouble – trouble in the big sense, but also trouble in terms of mental anxiety and stress. As Mark Twain says, "I've had a lot of worries in my life, most of which never happened." This is true for us personally, and in our relationships, so take a different path and assume positive intent in every situation. Give others the benefit of the doubt and share grace, and patience, and compassion, both with yourself and with the person you're interacting with, knowing that most often we have the best of intentions even when our execution falls short.

Reflect The Light Back

"I wish I could show you when you are lonely or in the darkness the astonishing light of your own being." – Hafiz of Persia

We all need friends, partners, colleagues, and family that can see the light in us even when we can't see it ourselves. As a result of being our own worst critics, it's understandable that we often lose sight of the light within ourselves, and this is true of the other people in our lives as well. For this reason it's critical to surround yourself with people who will see your light, and whose light you see, so you can reflect that light back when it becomes dim.

The best relationships in our life usually stem from our ability to reflect light back to those around us when they need it, and vice versa. We have the power to remind others of the light within them. This means encouraging each other when we are discouraged, when life gets us down, when we feel like we've failed, or when we've made decisions we wish we could undo. Reflecting the light is about lifting others up when they feel defined by their shortcomings, instead of as the whole of who they are.

This awareness is especially important at times when it feels like it is hard to see the light in others; this is when we must focus on the light and reflect it back. Remind the people in your life what you saw in them when you first met, why you connected, what greatness is within them, and what potential you still see. In doing so, we often give others permission to light up once again.

"Surround yourself with the dreamers and the doers, the believers and thinkers, but most of all, surround yourself with those who see the greatness within you, even when you don't see it yourself."
– Edmund Lee

Questions for Reflection:

How are you seeing the light in others?

What can you do today to recognize light in the people around you?

Is there a small way you can change how you treat someone, to treat them as if their light is all you see?

Where in your life do you find yourself regularly assuming negative intent, or negative results? What would it look like for you to assume positive intent in this situation, and respond based on that assumption?

Is there someone in your life whose light has grown dim, for whom you can take the opportunity to reflect light back to them?

CHAPTER 10

LOVE WITHOUT HOLDING BACK

"Go and love someone exactly as they are. And then watch how quickly they transform into the greatest, truest version of themselves. When one feels seen and appreciated in their own essence, one is instantly empowered." – Wes Angelozzi

When was the last time that you felt like the greatest, truest version of yourself? Sometimes it feels few and far between, doesn't it? I know there have been times when I've felt like it's been months, or years, since I felt that great about myself.

For me, that changed a few years ago. Two of my dearest friends have come from random encounters, during which we easily could have simply had a nice conversation and parted ways, but our conversations were deep and impactful and – dare I say it – lifechanging. With these friends, I regularly feel like the greatest and truest version of myself.

One of these encounters was through work, when I was assigned as the handler for a musician performing at an event. This is often a less than ideal job because, as glamorous as it may seem, catering to every whim of a musician often involves a lot of grunt work for very little reward. The event was taking place at the Museum of Fine Arts in Boston, and after set-up and sound check, I directed the musician to a small, elegantly set table in a grand rotunda that was surrounded by priceless works of art and advised the caterer to serve him dinner. At this moment, he invited me to join him, feeling out of place dining alone in such a grand space while he was on display for all the other vendors to see.

After receiving approval from my boss, I sat at the table – prepared to hear him regale me with stories about himself, or for pointless small talk. Within moments, instead, we were sharing our hearts about imposter syndrome, our dream jobs, and bucket lists for life – anything but mundane small talk. This one, relatively chance encounter has turned into a 5-year friendship where we converse on a weekly basis – all in the same vein as we did that night – no idle chitchat, always with stories and thoughts and experiences shared from the heart. And despite the fact that we only see each other once a year or so, usually for work, our friendship is one of those once-in-a-lifetime connections that we now couldn't imagine life without.

Sitting on an airplane en route from Boston to Chicago was where I made my other friend of a lifetime, over the span of a 2-hour flight. Seated across the aisle from me, an Israeli gentleman struck up a conversation – despite my best attempts to be otherwise engaged. It was one of those days where I didn't want to have a conversation with a stranger, and being stuck next to a talker on a flight was something I was dreading. Once again, though, the small talk was nowhere to be seen as we jumped right in to our thoughts on faith, favorite icons in the Bible (both of us being fans of David), and personal aspirations of writing a book. As has been the case with me and my musician friend, my Israeli friend and I have turned this one conversation (which happened four years ago) into a friendship in which we converse on a regular basis about our struggles, our hopes, our dreams, photo tours of our respective hometowns, and travels. Although, other than in that one in-person conversation, we have not crossed paths again physically, our lives have become intertwined.

There are a few key traits of these friendships which have allowed them to become two of my deepest, truest relationships, and they are traits I am trying to apply to all of the relationships in my life because I see the value and the way that these relationships have blossomed because of their unique nature. I have learned to love these two friends without holding back, and I want this to be something that defines all of my relationships. Here are the ways I have found work best in loving without holding back.

No Agenda

Relationships are most free to grow and blossom when you have no agenda for them. Can you recall the last time you invested in a relationship with absolutely zero agenda? It's hard, right? It means having a relationship with no expectation, no tit-for-tat, no measuring stick for how the relationship is performing or existing in your life. In approaching relationships this way, whether it is with a colleague, a parent, a spouse, your best friend or your neighbor, this approach allows the other person to show up fully as they are and then, as Wes Angelozzi says, to transform into the greatest, truest version of themselves.

Perhaps you are wondering what it means to have no agenda, or no expectation. Or you are thinking, how does that work with my spouse, or my colleague or employee, where expectation is an integral part of the relationship? This doesn't mean giving the other person a free pass to contribute nothing to the relationship, but it does mean allowing the person to show up as they are, in the best way they know how, and to contribute in the ways they best can and desire to.

There are so few relationships that exist without expectations. As a result, I constantly feel as though I'm letting people down, not being "enough" of whatever I think I am supposed to be for that person, and constantly measuring myself against a harsh standard of whether or not I am a good enough friend, spouse, daughter, neighbor, colleague, boss, or you name it. Granted, I admit I often put those expectations on myself, but they are derived from relationships in which I feel I have had or actually do have expectations to meet. As a result, these expectations impact the way I show up – which often is not as my best and truest self, but as the version of myself that has something to prove. On the contrary, the relationships which I feel have the lowest expectations for me to meet, where there is no agenda and I am loved simply for who I am, are the ones in which my truest and ultimately my best self shows up. And as a result, the other person gets the best and truest version of me.

Over the past few years I have seen my relationships evolve, and my closest, most important relationships are the ones in which I have the freedom to show up exactly as I am – with successes and failures to show, awesome traits and ugly ones alike – and be loved and accepted just as I am, and for who I am striving to be. And wow, am I so grateful for the people in my life who allow me to be me. And I want to be that person for everyone else in my life.

No Ego

In many ways loving without holding back means setting our ego aside. Our ego, as it relates to how we want others to see us, and our ego as it relates to how we see ourselves. It means letting ourselves be seen just as we are, flaws and all, good and bad and ugly and imperfectly beautiful. Setting our ego aside also means extending this grace, and forgiveness, and acceptance to others – just as they are.

I pride myself on being a lover of people, able to love people deeply and without restraint. My natural tendency has always been to love people – even people whom others find seemingly unlovable. But it hasn't always come with ease. Loving people can be hard, and messy, and incredibly disappointing and hurtful at times. And every time I am knocked down because someone has seemingly taken advantage of my love, or taken me for granted, or disappointed me, or deliberately hurt me, I have to pause and re-evaluate, asking myself, "Is this really worth it?" Wouldn't it be much easier to just keep my distance, to not love as much, or to only love when that love is perfectly reciprocated? Ultimately, I always decide that yes, this practice of unconditional love is really worth it, but it is a conscious and deliberate choice I have to make on an ongoing basis.

Pride is often what gets in the way of our ability to love others without restraint. We take offense when someone doesn't respond the way we think they should. Or after calling, or texting, and getting no response, we decide to hold off and not call, text, or reach out the next time for fear of bruising our ego with another lack of response. Or we temper the effusiveness of our love to match the other person's level exactly, to protect ourselves from being vulnerable or seeming foolish for expressing too much love and care. And I get it, it's hard to be vulnerable and express love that might not be returned. But expressing it is so much better than the alternative. Our world needs more love. We need more people who are willing share their hearts and compassion and their light, regardless of the outcome.

To love without holding back means to share your love without keeping score, without worrying if you have received love from a person, without reserving your expressions of love only for when love is returned and affirmed. For me, it means setting aside my fear of vulnerability, and my concern about how something will be perceived, and telling my friends I love them regularly – often even if we've just met. For me, it means texting regularly to tell someone they are on my mind, that I'm praying for them, that this quote or this item has made me think of them, even if I haven't had a response – because what harm is there in someone knowing that they are loved and cared for? And chances are, if they aren't responding it's because life is hectic, and challenging, and stressful, and a little extra love can go a long way. And, if by chance, it means they don't really value our friendship or my expression of love, what harm has been done? It certainly doesn't diminish the value of the love I've shared. So, check your ego at the door.

Spreading love is always a good idea.

Be Fully Present

"The most precious gift we can offer others is our presence. When mindfulness embraces those we love, they will bloom like flowers."
– Thich Nhat Hanh

To truly share love, and love without holding back, we need to be fully present. Loving without holding back doesn't come when we are on our phones, reading email, or checking the news at the dinner table. Loving without holding back doesn't come when we are lost in our own thoughts, scanning a room for something to distract us, or preparing our response without fully listening to what another person has to say. Loving without holding back comes from being fully present.

I know that what I share with people in my life is often a direct result of how present they are in our conversation. I am someone who would always rather have someone else talking than speak myself. But when I have someone's undivided attention, when they have given me the gift of their presence, I will share my deepest thoughts and feelings. I will open myself up to vulnerability and tell stories, share my fears, and offer insights. Those who offer me their presence experience a version of me that is also fully present. I've seen my own response to being fully present, and I try to practice this in my relationships as well. Being fully present has allowed me to love without holding back. And often, I can't love without agenda or ego unless I am fully present in the moment, and giving permission for the other person to do the same.

Try loving without holding back. I promise, it will change your life.

Questions for Reflection:

Is there anyone in your life who you love without holding back?

What would it look like, for you, to love others without agenda, ego, or distraction?

In what small way can you change your habits, in order to be fully present in your relationships today?

PART 2: SECTION 3

OPTIMISM & COMMUNITY

Optimism cannot exist in isolation, because our lives do not occur in isolation. Therefore, to live and practice optimism, we must also practice it in the way we view and the way we interact with our community. Community has a significant impact on who we are and how we view the world, and we have the ability to influence and shape the communities in which we are a part of.

Community can mean many things. A group of people living in the same place or having a particular characteristic in common, or a feeling of fellowship with others as a result of sharing something in common, be it a location, attitude, interest, or goals.

For the purposes of these next few chapters, we will talk about community in various forms, as detailed below.

The inner circle. This is the community that we have created, which is made up of the people who are closest to us, those with whom we interact on a daily and regular basis in close and intimate ways. Our immediate family, our closest friends, our confidants at work. These are the people who, either by blood or by choice, we choose to keep close and to share our life with most closely.

The immediate community. This is the community which, being one step removed from the inner circle, is most often created by our circumstances. This community involves the people with whom we share a location, be it our neighborhood or town, the congregation at the church we attend, our division at work, or where we volunteer.

The world. This is community in the grandest sense of the word. The community that exists as a result of our identifying with a particular nationality or way of life, of our being part of a community of believers, of our being a part of the human race.

We live in a time in which our communities are struggling. From the overwhelming epidemic of loneliness, to the technological advances that allow us to keep interactions with others at a minimum, to the inexplicable violence that is occurring in our schools and on the world stage, now more than ever we need people who are influencers of hope, peace, connection, and possibility.

In these next few chapters we are going to dive into what it means to influence your communities with optimism. We will discuss the ways to bring optimism to your inner circle, your immediate community, and the world. It is time that we built a world of optimism.

CHAPTER 11

SURROUND YOURSELF WITH PEOPLE WHO CHALLENGE YOU TO GROW

"You are the average of the five people you spend the most time with, so choose wisely." – Jim Rohn

The saying above is one that I find to be true, but also challenging and a bit nerve-wracking at the same time. Whether the concept is based on only and exactly the top five people we spend our time with, regardless of how we define "spending time," the spirit of the sentiment is the same. Simply, the people whom you spend time with have an impact on your life.

Who are the people that have an impact on your life, that shape who you are and how you see the world? Do they help you to be more optimistic? Do they bring about your pessimistic side? What about the influence you have on others? Are you sharing a mindset of hope and possibility?

To practice a life of optimism, we must surround ourselves with people who challenge us to grow.

I'm currently in the middle of another life transition. I am shifting my career once again as I strive to share my message on optimism with the world through my book, workshops and retreats, speaking engagements, a blog, and any other way I can possibly shout optimism from the rooftops. In reflecting on my life, and my community, I realized about a year ago that I was incredibly well-equipped for the life I was living. I am surrounded by people who love and accept me as I am, I have great friends, colleagues and mentors who have helped my event planning business grow to amazing heights, and I have people who challenge me to volunteer more and to learn new hobbies. But in terms of moving into a new role as an author and speaker, part of that realization was that my community could be enhanced. While my husband, my mother, and my best friend are the biggest cheerleaders and advocates for my dreams and goals, none of them have the knowledge or skill-set needed to know how to write a book, give a Ted talk, or share an idea on the world stage.

What is your community like? Have you surrounded yourself with people who challenge you to grow? Or do you find yourself comfortable in the status quo, with communities that are satisfied with the status quo as well?

For me, as I assessed where I wanted to go in the next few years, personally and professionally, I started exploring ways to grow my community with people who could challenge, inspire, and mentor me in this new phase of life. I found myself joining a mastermind group – this is a group of other professionals intended to challenge and support growth in our businesses and lives. This particular group is comprised of twelve women who are seeking to make a bold difference in the world through sharing their own unique message, in their own unique way; be it as a thought leader, a coach, an author, a speaker, they are all agents of change in their communities and in the world. Within this group, I have found peers and mentors who provide life experience for me to learn from, questions and nudges which encourage me to view life and my goals and my position from a new light, collaborators with whom I have embarked on new projects, friends who have counseled me in difficult times of transition and self-doubt, and mentors who have previously paved the path I am trying to pave. Since I have joined it, this group has evolved to comprise new, dear close friends who are part of my inner circle, an immediate community in which I exist as part of a group sharing goals and beliefs, and a community in which I can exist, and collaborate, to help change the world.

In no way does this new group replace the existing communities that I have, but the individuals within it enhance and supplement my community as I grow and change and evolve. And I am better for having people who know my roots, know personally and deeply where I have been and where I'm coming from, and now to have people who are helping me to grow towards what I want to become.

Have you surrounded yourself with people who challenge you to grow? What does that look like for you? Do you challenge others?

In my experience, surrounding ourselves with people who challenge us to grow comes in a few key ways.

Don't Be the Smartest Person in the Room

This maxim is traditionally used in relation to intelligence and being the smartest in a group, but I would apply this to other traits also, such as kindness, courage, compassion, faith, and any number of traits and skills that we aspire to exemplify in our lives. In all aspects of our lives, we need to surround ourselves with people who are examples of what we would like to become. We should surround ourselves with those who help give us optimism, and faith, so that we can reach that goal of who we want to become. People whom we can emulate and learn from. People who are beacons for the type of person we want to become.

In our inner circles, this might mean having a friend or spouse who is your example of kindness or courage. In our immediate communities, perhaps it is the neighbor that teaches you more about compassion and giving back, or it is the community leader who has the historical knowledge from which you can learn more about improving your city. On the world stage, maybe it is the thought leader whose books you read and whose podcast you enjoy. Wherever the source, near or far, surround yourself with people who are smarter, braver, kinder, more courageous, more compassionate, and different from yourself – and learn from them.

Find People Who Speak the Truth, and Listen

Although we all love to have people agree with us and tell us how wonderful our thoughts and ideas are, this is not a successful recipe for growth. We need people who will speak truth into our lives, and they need to be people whom we respect and, as a result, will listen to. Without people who will speak the truth, and challenge us, our growth will come more slowly – or perhaps not at all. When we are listening to advice, encouragement, and sometimes a good kick in the pants from people whose advice we value, we are more apt to initiate and sustain change that helps us grow and change for the better.

As part of the process of writing this book, I have needed to ask for feedback on countless occasions. As a perfectionist, I wanted to get my draft perfect from the get-go before asking for help, but that isn't quite realistic. And ultimately, I don't want people in my life who love me but won't be truthful with me. I've asked friends and colleagues, mentors and experts, strangers, and people who love me the most, to give me feedback – to speak truth to me. In some cases, this has meant I've heard some hard truths – hearing about something that didn't quite resonate in what I'd written or done, something that didn't make sense (at all!), or something I wrote that had offended the reader. In every case, though, I believe (and hope!) that the feedback has made me better and stronger, and that I have grown as a result of that feedback.

Whether it's in regard to a project such as this book, about how I present myself in this world, or about knowledge, lifestyle, or belief, I hope I will always be surrounded by people who will speak truth to me – who will tell me when I'm being short-sighted, when I'm not living up to my potential, or when I've hurt feelings – people who will challenge me to grow. By growing into more of who I want to be, and a better person overall, I am then more equipped to make a positive difference in my communities and in the world.

Learn From Everyone

Some of our communities we get to choose for ourselves, and some are a matter of our circumstances or just the fact that we are human, surrounded by other humans. While the first two suggestions noted above for surrounding yourself with people who challenge you to grow are based upon choosing and building your community, I do believe there is still growth that can occur from the communities which we are a part of without choice having been involved, and which we wouldn't want to choose. Whether we're talking about a difficult boss, an annoying neighbor, a politician we vehemently disagree with, or a family member we struggle to love, I think there is something that we can learn from everyone. Sometimes it's a lesson in patience – the type of lesson I particularly despise. Sometimes it's a lesson in compassion or trust or letting go.

Part of building optimism in your life, and in your community, is being able to glean lessons from unexpected, and often unwelcomed, places. And people are often the instigators of such lessons. So, as you surround yourself with people who challenge you to grow, remember that even the people you haven't chosen for yourself can be opportunities for growth.

Questions for Reflection:

Who in your life challenges you to grow? In what way?

Do you have people in your life who speak truth to you? How do you respond to truth-telling?

Are there people in your life who are particularly difficult parts of your community? What can you learn from them?

How can you surround yourself with more people who challenge you to grow?

CHAPTER 12

MOTIVATE CHANGE

"Never doubt that a small group of thoughtful, committed citizens can change the world; indeed, it's the only thing that ever has." – Margaret Mead

Change is inevitable. There is change that is forced and change that is inspired. The change that comes from motivation and inspiration always seems more palatable than the change that is forced, and creates lasting impact in individuals, communities, and the world.

Where is change occurring in your life right now? Are you being motivated to pursue and embrace that change, or is it feeling forced in your life? Are you instigating change in your own life?

Since I was a teenager, I knew that I wanted to be a force for change. In high school I was invited to join the Youth Board of Directors for the United Way in my community. This was one of my first exposures to non-profits, and being involved – at a leadership level – with the United Way would shape my perspective on being a change agent in the community, as well as instill in me the importance of working for change in the world.

One of the first non-profit gigs my newfound company was hired for put me in the role of project and event manager. Not only would I be involved in the event logistics, which were where my most recent experience had been specialized, but I'd been hired to oversee the management of the project as a whole. Project management in this case was no easy feat, as I was coming in during a time of significant turn-over for the organization. I was responsible for bringing together all of the full-time staff members who worked on the project, a disjointed committee, as well as the top level sponsors in order to accomplish the increased and improved fundraising goals. Of course I also needed to execute a flawless event at a level the organization had not previously accomplished. The infighting in the organization was mind-blowing – the sponsors didn't respect the staff, the staff disagreed with the committee, and working with the committee (as with many committees) was like herding cats. Yet they all agreed on one thing – they did not want an outsider coming in to force change for their event and their organization. I have to admit, I came to dread this event as I worked toward it, and I wanted to quit on countless occasions. But I didn't. I mustered every bit of strength and wisdom I had to try and motivate change.

In the end, the celebratory event debriefing spoke wonders, for we all sat around – staff, committee and sponsors – and shared our highlights from the event. There were a number of challenges and event logistics that did not go seamlessly, and there were a lot of lessons learned, but the sense of community we built was a success. The committee cohesively agreed on what had been a success and areas for improvement, the sponsors praised the staff with specificity and effusiveness, and the staff aligned with the vision the committee and sponsors collectively set forth for the new year. I do not take credit for the changes that occurred in the interaction of the group or for the success of the event, but I do think I helped motivate the change and create a foundation for the growth and improved sense of community to occur.

What does it mean for you to work for change in your communities – whether it is in your inner circle, such as your immediate family or relationships, or on a larger scale in your neighborhood, workplace, or in the world? Do you associate change with positive improvement, as a influence for good? Do you believe that you can be an agent for change, and make a difference in your communities?

Here are my top tips for how you can motivate change in your own communities.

Share Your Vision

> *"Where there is no vision, there is no hope."*
> *– George Washington Carver*

Too many of us have a vision for how to change the world, or how to make things better in our workplaces and our communities, but we remain silent. Our silence stems from fear of failure or vulnerability, and the assumption that our idea will be dismissed or disregarded; we worry that people will think we are crazy or tell us all the reasons that it can't be done. But that is exactly why we need people who speak up and who share their vision with others. Without a vision of how our inner circle, our families, our workplaces, and our communities can improve, we will remain stuck in the status quo.

Sharing your vision is an opportunity to bring people together, to remind others to believe in possibility and see what possibility exists. Speak up. Speak your truth for what you want for the communities in which you live and thrive. Give others a vision they can latch on to and work towards.

Perhaps your vision is more time with family and loved ones. How can you share that vision and paint a picture of what it looks like to have a family vacation, or a day together at the beach, or time spent volunteering together? Maybe you have a vision for a neighborhood garden or playground, a place in which your immediate community can come together. Many of us have a vision for a safer world which translates to safer schools, safer cities, safer travel. How can you share your vision with others, and invite them to join you on the journey towards making that vision a reality?

Lead By Example

"The world is changed by your example, not by your opinion."
– Paulo Coelho

Sharing your vision must be backed up by you acting on your vision. No one will buy into your vision for change unless you are actively working towards that change yourself. You must believe in your vision, regardless of what everyone else says or believes, and take advantage of every effort to implement your vision for change. Your actions are what will inspire others to come alongside. If you are working hard, they will be inspired to work hard. If you are relentless in pursuit of your passion, your passion will be contagious. If you are tackling obstacles head on, moving forward through failure, and refusing to be deterred, then others will do the same. Action and example is the greatest way to motivate change in your community, in others, and in the world.

In the examples noted in the prior section about sharing your vision, how can you lead by example? If you want more time with your family, what can you do to schedule that time together with family and loved ones? What plans can you put in place to make it both a priority and a reality? In the case of a neighborhood garden or playground, what steps can you take to lay the groundwork for bringing that to fruition? If you want a safer world, what are you doing to support and enhance more safety in your communities at every level?

Empower

"The ultimate use of power is to empower others."
– William Glasser

Truly sustainable, transformational change occurs when we can empower others to create change. While it is important for us to motivate change in others by sharing a vision for change and leading by example, the change will not extend beyond ourselves until other people are inspired and empowered to rise up for change themselves. It is not only important that you are motivating the change you envisioned, but that you are empowering others to share their own vision, to lead by example, and to empower others, as well. Motivating change is about paying it forward, about the domino effect that occurs when we instigate change in one corner of our community, and it changes the world.

In our inner circle or family structure it might mean giving our children the freedom to pick how we spend free time together on the weekend, or picking the activity we share together after dinner. In our immediate communities, empowering others might mean creating opportunities for others to lead or spearhead the direction of that neighborhood garden, by helping to select the location, set-up the garden structure, or even create their own mini-neighborhood garden on their own street. In the larger context of the world, empowering others can mean giving others a voice to be heard, having a vote towards how something is handled, or providing resources of time or money or connections in ways that can support others in making change.

When we motivate positive change in the world, it contributes to building a world of optimism. It spreads the message of hope and belief in possibility, in something better and improved, and it creates a platform for making those improvements a reality. How do you want to motivate change in the world?

Questions for Reflection:

What vision do you have? Have you shared it with others?

In what ways do you lead by example? What steps can you take to turn your vision into action, and set an example for others?

What does it mean to you to empower others? How are you empowering those in your inner circle, in your immediate community, and in the world?

CHAPTER 13

LEAVE THE WORLD A BIT BETTER

"To laugh often and much; to win the respect of intelligent people and the affection of children; to earn the appreciation of honest critics and endure the betrayal of false friends; to appreciate beauty; to find the best in others; to leave the world a bit better, whether by a healthy child, a garden patch or a redeemed social condition; to know that even one life has breathed easier because you have lived. This is to have succeeded." – Ralph Waldo Emerson

It's challenging to say anything more meaningful than what Emerson has expressed here. My favorite part of this quote is: "leave the world a bit better". For as long as I can recall, this has been my favorite quote on success, and has driven the way I view not only success, but the ways in which I can make an impact on the world. The ways that we can leave the world a bit better are countless, and all incredibly important. This is especially the case in uncertain times, which seem more and more prevalent with each passing year. As uncertainty, negativity, and despair seem to prevail, we need people who are working for clarity, positivity, and solutions that leave our world better.

Right now you might be thinking that life is so crazy, how can you possibly change the world. And I recognize that so often we think of making a difference in the world as something that is grand and global – the way the Gates Foundation or Oprah work to leave the world better. But that is the beauty of this quote by Emerson, and the reality of what it means to leave the world a bit better – it doesn't have to be on a grand global scale. Changing the world, and leaving it better, can start with one person, one small square of soil, one idea.

As much as I have measured success in my life by this quote of Emerson's, my father is who has instilled in me a sense of success that is measured by how I have helped others, or helped even one other person. My father, an optimist and believer of possibilities, believes we all have a duty to improve the world by helping others – and it starts simply with the people who cross our paths.

"On this journey of life, let your success be measured by how you lighten the load of your neighbor, your fellow traveler. Your neighbor, however, is not necessarily the person living in the house next to you, but rather the person that crosses your path today."
– JB

A few years ago, my family was vacationing together in Sedona, Arizona. One of the long-anticipated highlights of our trip was the afternoon where we'd be renting Jeeps to go rock crawling in the Red Rocks. This is an iconic Sedona experience, and my brother, husband and I were competing over who would be able to drive first. Behind us in line at the car rental agency was a couple in their late-40s conversing in German. My father, never one to know a stranger and also conversant in German, struck up a conversation with the couple from Berlin. As we received the keys to our Jeep and started to depart, my father overheard the couple being denied a rental because they could not prove their car insurance was valid in the United States. Their disappointment was apparent, as they had anticipated this activity as much as we had. At that moment, my father stepped in and asked the rental agent if he rented the Jeep with his insurance verification, could our new friends from Germany drive? Perplexed by the entire situation of a stranger helping a stranger, the agent agreed. So, off we went in two Jeeps, instead of one, accompanied by our newfound friends.

Following the Jeep outing, we shared beers and appetizers with our friends from Berlin, and subsequently kept in touch. The following summer, their son spent a month living in Idaho with my parents. Three years later, we spent Christmas in Berlin, celebrating Christmas dinner in their home with their extended family. As we sat around the table after our Christmas meal, we reflected back on the original meeting in Sedona and how one small action creates a ripple effect. Our German friends shared that now, due to that encounter in Sedona, they look for other opportunities to help strangers. As a result of that day where my father stepped forward and invested in a stranger, and used his time and financial resources to help, they too have adopted a mindset of helping strangers, of being mindful of how they can lighten the load of the fellow traveler that crosses their path on any given day.

As Emerson eloquently states, leaving the world a bit better can range from you affecting a child's life, on to a garden, to an improved social condition. I've taken Emerson's poignant words, and my father's philosophy on life, to exemplify what it means to leave the world a bit better. Having a positive impact on the world, on my communities that extend from my inner circle, to my immediate networks, and to the world as a whole, is one of the ways in which I share my optimism with the world. Optimism is about seeing the best that is possible, and in leaving the world a bit better I am practicing the practical optimism of making that best possible more of a reality.

What do you think of when you reflect on making the world better for your inner circle – your immediate family, friends, and loved ones? How can you leave the world a bit better as it relates to your network – your neighborhood, your workplace, your church or local organizations? What does it mean to you to leave the world a bit better?

In my efforts to leave the world a bit better, these are the paths I have found that make the most significant impact, and help me reach the level of success laid out by Emerson and my father.

Invest In People

"I've learned that people will forget what you said, people will forget what you did, but people will never forget how you made them feel." – Maya Angelou

We have the opportunity, and the power, to make a profound impact on people's lives. The first and most profound way of doing that is to invest in people, and to leave people for the better. May we be known for lightening another's load, for bringing joy to others, and for helping others to be the best versions of themselves. For you, maybe investing in people means raising a healthy child who will contribute to the world. To my father, investing in people means that there is no such thing as a stranger. For teachers, this mindset best points to the students whose minds and educations they help shape. For me, it means loving people deeply and intensely, and helping them to see that they are full of potential and possibility while also being amazing and enough already, just as they are.

Who are the people that have made the deepest impact on your life, who have left your world a bit better? I'd guess that these are the people who have invested in you the most – with their time, their energy, and their belief in who you are and support of what you do. What investments have others made in you that you treasure the most? What does it look like for you to invest in others?

Use Your Resources

We all have resources that can be used to leave the world a bit better. Time, money, and connections are just a few of the resources that we have at our disposal to help us impact the world. Making use of them can be straightforward, in the way that non-profits value contributions by their board members: donate your money, volunteer your time, or connect us with people who will do those things. But it doesn't have to be that formulaic. Leaving the world better, through your resources, can mean shoveling the walkway for your neighbor, taking time to teach your nephew how to drive, buying a hot meal for the homeless person on the street, or using your voice – or platform – to raise awareness about a cause. Although your resources might not look like everyone else's, it makes them all the more valuable. You always have something to give – some way that you can contribute. Find ways to give back and to make your world, your community, better.

What resources are most readily available to you? Is there a skill set or talent you have that is easy for you to share? Do you have time to help your family and friends, your neighbors, or volunteer on a local committee? Are there resources you have now that you feel aren't being utilized to their fullest potential? What would it look like for you to maximize your resources in order to leave the world a bit better?

Share Your Ideas, Beliefs, and Values

Spreading our ideas, beliefs, and values is the final way I've seen that we can improve the world. As Emerson states it in his quote on success, it is about leaving a redeemed social condition. As my father sees it, it's sharing his vision, his belief that we should help our fellow traveler along the way. It could be sharing your faith with someone who is searching for answers, or perhaps it is about instilling positive values in your children that they can then pass on to their children. For me, it's all about optimism, and sharing faith and hope and belief in possibility with others.

Do you believe that your ideas, your beliefs, and your values can make an impact on the world? What does it look like for you to share your ideas and values, and leave the world a bit better as a result?

Remember, changing the world does not have to be a global cause that you champion for today, although the world definitely needs people for that as well. Changing the world can be about helping your family, leaving your neighborhood better than you found it, supporting a cause that your friend is passionate about, or giving time to your local community.

Leave the world a bit better, because one baby step or one giant leap at a time, you have the power to change the world.

Questions for Reflection:

How can you leave your community – your inner circle, your immediate community, and the world – a bit better?

In what ways are you investing in people? Who can you invest in today?

How are you using your resources, your time, or your money to contribute to your communities?

In what ways are you sharing your ideas, beliefs, and values in order to make the world a bit better?

PART 2: SECTION 4

OPTIMISM & SELF

" It is not the mountain we conquer but ourselves."
– Edmund Hillary

Perhaps you are wondering why I saved the section about optimism and self until the end. It seems like one of the most important, the most integral, right? I also think that optimism, as it relates to ourselves, can be the most difficult thing to practice. From an outside perspective, it is often easy to believe in the unlimited potential of others, to believe in possibility for the community and the world, but looking inward, it can be a struggle to have that same lens of hope and faith and possibility for ourselves and our own potential.

And yet, optimism as it relates to ourselves is the most important, because it is almost impossible to be optimistic about external circumstances if we cannot also be optimistic about our internal state of being.

As we've seen in the prior sections, optimism is critical to every aspect of ourselves. In our work optimists have more satisfaction and success. In relationships optimists have more meaningful, healthy, and fulfilling interactions. In our communities, optimists are the ones who believe that positive change is possible and make it so.

In relation to ourselves, optimism leads to more fulfilling, successful, and vibrant lives. In this section we are going to explore what it means to live an optimistic life as it relates to ourselves, and how to look at our personal lives with optimism in order to live a more inspired life.

CHAPTER 14

WHO YOU ARE IS MORE IMPORTANT THAN WHAT YOU DO

"Happiness is not about doing, it's about being."
–Richard Branson

"You're a cool lady." Exactly what every 30 year old woman wants to hear. This was something that makes me akin to my feisty, exuberant grandmother who no one could get enough of. Don't get me wrong, I see it as a complement, even if it's a quirky one that makes me feel 90-years-old, but still one which makes me smile to this day.

It was a hot May day when I attended a community dinner in Brooklyn at the then-headquarters of Holstee. True to the Holstee Manifesto, for which Holstee is most well-known for, this community dinner was more of an intimate gathering of friends than a don't-know-anyone-yet type networking dinner party. The gathering embodied the sentiments of the Holstee Manifesto. "Open your mind, arms and heart to new things and people" was a hallmark of the night, and "Ask the next person you see what their passion is, and share your inspiring dream with them" may as well have been the handbook for the evening's conversation. I met exceptional, inspiring people with diverse passions, and they left me feeling passionate, hopeful, and deeply touched by the generosity of spirit and light bursting forth from the dreams in the room.

What I appreciated most about the evening, and the conversations stemming from it, was that no one ever asked, "What do you do?" In this group of people, it was a given that who you are is much more important than what you do, so the conversations were focused around who you are being, and not what you are doing.

Recall the last time you were in a social situation meeting new people; how many times did the question of "what do you do?" come up? Can you think of a time you were at a networking event where you weren't asked what you do, or where you didn't ask others what they do? It's rare. So often it seems like where we live and what we do are what most defines us. And yet we are so much more than what we do.

Remembering that we are more than what we do is a key part of looking at ourselves optimistically, in seeing ourselves as the whole being, and recognizing that we are multi-faceted, diverse beings that cannot be defined simply by one aspect of how we spend our time.

If you had to share yourself only in terms of who you are, not what you do, do you know what you would share? To take this challenge of how we see ourselves to the next level, if you had to share who you are in and of yourself, not as you relate to other people (such as through you being a child, friend, or spouse), do you know how you would speak of yourself?

It took me years to remember who I am, in and of myself. I am an optimist (of course!). I am curious, passionate, inspired, and driven. I'm a woman of faith. I'm a traveler and explorer, I'm a helper, I'm a bit whimsical and silly at times, and I'm overly serious at others. I am creative, although it took me a long time to embrace this aspect of myself because I'm not a traditional artist or musician. I'm thoughtful and kind and warm and sometimes funny. And I'm a dreamer. I am also a daughter, an aunt, a wife, a friend, a boss, a colleague, a sister, a granddaughter, a member of a church, a Bostonian, an American, and an Italian (at heart at least).

Who are you? Take a moment and reflect, remember who you were as a child, remember who you are at your core, remember what defines you, what makes you unique, what makes you, you.

The most impactful conversation on that May night came from my "cool lady" friend. In speaking about our passions, he shared with me his "Daily Leaven" or "Daily Eleven"… depending on how you heard it. I heard it as "Daily Leaven", which was fitting since leaven causes things to expand and rise, although he did mean it as the "Daily Eleven". This is a list of the things he wants to work towards every day in order to be most fulfilled and content, the things which lift his spirits and help him to grow into the person he is trying to become. Items such as Gratitude, Health, Volunteering, and Family made his list of what makes for a good day.

I was inspired. What would my "Daily Leaven" look like? I reflected on what is important to me and created my own list, which has remained the same since that first draft I wrote almost four years ago now. I lovingly refer to this as my: TO BE ME list. What fills my cup to the point of overflowing? What makes me the best version of myself? In what state of being do

I find that I have the most joy and fulfillment in my life? For me and my list, I chose to pursue broader concepts, feelings and states of being that encapsulate how I want to relate to and experience life. I did not want this to become another inflexible to-do list that couldn't adjust with a busy, ever-changing life. This was to be lasting.

This is what my list includes:

Be Still
Be Grateful
Be Curious
Be Active
Be Productive
Be Expressive
Be Connected
Be Silly
Be Giving
Be Restored
Be Inspired

If you were to write your own TO BE list, what would it include? What are the states of being that give you the most joy and fulfillment? What encapsulates how you want to experience life?

My list has helped me stay grounded in who I am, instead of simply in what I do. This grounding helps me to view myself and my life more optimistically, because I recognize what I am passionate about, what makes me more complete, and I have created a flexible structure in which to be more of these things each day.

As I continue to reflect on my TO BE ME list, and try to navigate every day what it means to really be me, I've found that there are three key areas to evaluate when you are identifying who you are, and who you want to be.

In And Of Yourself

As I asked already, who are you? Not as it relates to anyone else, but as the question relates to you – personally, deeply? Being able to define this is imperative to being able to live as a person who is being, rather than a person who is simply doing. What are the traits that you love about yourself, that you want to be known for? What are the traits you want to explore and embody? What about you is part of who you are, but perhaps could be improved?

For instance, I am a perfectionist – it's a part of who I am that I don't particularly love, and which I'm trying to change. But I love and appreciate that I am driven; it's part of what has made so much in my life possible. And I love that I'm a dreamer. If people knew nothing else about me, I'd probably be happy if this was the one thing they knew.

If people knew nothing else about you, what would you want them to know about who you are?

In Relation To Others

The ways we relate to other people is a huge part of what defines us. There are the titles – the things that are some combination of being and doing – such as daughter, employee, and friend. And then there is being in relation to other people. I love to be helpful. I love to be an instigator of conversation, and sometimes tough conversations. I love to be inspirational. And being silly is much more fun with others than it is alone. There are also some things, like being kind, that can be part of you in and of yourself, but don't have the value or meaning without their being related to other people.

Who are you in relation to others? Who do you want to be as it relates to others?

In Your Legacy

I also think there is a lasting part of who we are that is important for us to define and reflect upon. Legacy is simply what will be handed down. What are we leaving for others, for the future? Are you a consumer only – taking from the world and not giving back? Or are you a contributor? Are you being expressive, and sharing your art or your gifts with the world? Are you being a visionary and leaving a legacy of thoughtful change?

Leaving a legacy does not have to be about what you've done, but about who you have been and how that has impacted others, and the world, in a lasting way.

As you learn what it means to be defined by who you are, instead of what you do, I encourage you to reflect on things that define what makes you fully you… write out the statements of who you are, and create your own TO BE ME list, one that inspires you, fills your cup, helps you reset when a day is going down a less than ideal path, and which gives you peace and fulfillment as another day ticks by.

Questions for Reflection:

"Can you remember who you were, before the world told you who you should be?" – Charles Bukowski

What are you most proud of being?

What does it look like for you to be known for who you are and not what you do?

CHAPTER 15

BUILD YOUR LIFE AROUND WHAT MATTERS MOST

"Things which matter most must never be at the mercy of things which matter least." – Johann Wolfgang von Goethe

My mother is a remarkable woman. She is the woman whom I most admire, and whom I most aspire to be like in my life. There is not a book long enough for the ways in which I respect my mother. I hope someday that I will have even a glimmer of the love, faith, compassion, hope and grace that she embodies. She is one of the defining reasons that I am an optimist, and live optimistically towards myself and others.

Although I have felt this way about my mother for a long time, while I was growing up there was one trait I saw in my mother that I just as clearly said I would never emulate – I viewed her as a workaholic. I recall family vacations to Seattle or California where my mother would be in the hotel room working away while the rest of us were exploring the city. One trip in particular during a college break, my mother, grandmother, and I were en route to Sun Valley, Idaho, which was about a 3-hour drive from our home in Boise. On the drive, my grandmother and I had to sit in silence while my mother carried on nonstop conference calls. I was livid, and did nothing to hide my frustration and my anger with my mother. I recall throwing a temper tantrum and attempting to throw my mom's cell phone to a place of no return. Not my finest moment. But at that time, I promised myself that when I got older, that would never be me. I would never choose work over time with family.

And yet I recall, vividly, that Thanksgiving morning, four years ago, where I was overwhelmed with an upcoming event and needed to work. I felt that I had so much work to do that, when my mother came into the office and wanted to chat, connect, and spend time with me, I responded by saying something like "Do you need something? I don't have time right now." Although these weren't my exact words, what I felt like I was saying was, "I don't have time for you." And I was stopped dead in my tracks. In that moment, every time my mother had worked on vacation while I'd been growing up flashed before my eyes, my promise to myself to never reach that point echoing in my mind, and here was the moment of self-crisis, with me thinking: I have become exactly what I said I never would.

I am glad to say that my mother, being a gracious, understanding, and loving woman, did not take that moment personally (even though I certainly did), and it didn't impact our relationship in the long run. But it is still a moment I reflect on often, and I use it to remind myself of this:

I want to build a life around what matters most.

I fully recognize that, even if I'd focused on building a life around what matters most, that exact scenario with my mother might still have happened. And they can mutually exist –

103

even at times when it seems like we have mastered building a life around what matters most, it's possible we might still be pressed for time or stressed about work. But I know deep down that in that moment, my life was not built around what mattered most. My life, in that moment, was built around creating a successful business and doing everything I could to exceed the expectations of my clients at the expense of taking care of myself, nourishing important relationships, and finding ways to be personally fulfilled. And I would really like to say that, as a result of that moment, I used it as a turning point in my life and I made immediate and impactful changes so that, by the next Thanksgiving, I was rocking out my life built around what mattered most. But that wasn't the case, either. It took me a few years to shift my thinking and build my life around what mattered most.

First, it took me identifying what really mattered most. I thought I knew, but you certainly wouldn't have known it based on my actions, based on how I spent my time and invested my energy. Next, it took understanding what it meant to prioritize it. It took learning what is non-negotiable and what I am not willing to sacrifice no matter what. And it took sharing that with other people, and creating structures that honor and reflect what I espouse.

Building a life around what matters most is key to living optimistically, because what matters most ultimately brings us the most joy, the most positivity, and the most fulfillment in our lives.

Here are the key tips I've discovered in re-building my life around what matters most.

ELIZABETH SHAW

Identify What Matters Most

"Be true to what matters most to your heart."
– Cheryl Richardson

If I were to ask you right now what matters most to you, I'm sure you'd have a quick response for me… either a response that is an honest reflection of your life now, or a response that is what you think you're supposed to say but may not be exactly what is true. For me, connecting with people is what matters most – but that Thanksgiving, I'm sure no one would have believed it. A friend of mine's first response was that his top priority is building his business, although on closer reflection, he says that this isn't really what ultimately matters to him the most… it's just where he invests most of his time and energy, because building his business allows him to take care of his family and loved ones in the way he desires, with the ultimate goal of having more time and resources for them.

Identifying what matters most is a process that requires digging deep into what resonates most in the inner corners of your heart. It means a lot of difficult conversations with yourself about what you want, what you're willing to sacrifice, and about the life you want to create. Ask yourself the tough questions – what will you regret not doing or being or prioritizing in your life? Look at all aspects of your life – faith, career, family, relationships, self, and education. Factor it all in. And then prioritize it. For some people, this is a lifelong prioritization – what you determine now as most important will always be most important-, yet, for others, the prioritization will only be for this season of life and then change in the future. Either way is okay, or you can do both and have two separate sets of priorities, if it helps you maintain clarity about what

105

matters most to you. And reevaluate it regularly, because priorities change. For example, investing in your children's lives isn't usually a priority until you've had children, or working extra hours to buy a house might be a priority only for a short season of your life.

What is tugging at your heart right now? When you think about what matters most, do you have clarity about what is most important to you?

As you clarify what matters most to you, don't let it exist only in your mind. Write it down. Create a vision statement which can be a guiding light for what you want from your life and how you want to live your life. Document a list of your priorities. Something that you can set on your desk, or put in your wallet, or stare at in your mirror every morning to remind yourself what matters most. Having a clear vision will help you to remember what matters most, and focus your energy as you build your life around it.

Know Your Non-Negotiables

"You have to decide what your highest priorities are and have the courage - pleasantly, smilingly, and non-apologetically - to say 'no' to other things. And the way to do that is by having a bigger 'yes' burning inside of you." – Stephen Covey

Now that you've prioritized what matters most in your life, determine what is non-negotiable. What are you not willing to sacrifice? At one point in my life, it was being home for dinner every night with my husband. For a friend of mine, it is self-care in the form of at least seven hours of sleep every night. A woman from my church will not sacrifice at least 30 minutes for prayer and reading her Bible each morning. For this season of my life, my non-negotiable is time to write every morning before I do anything else. For my husband, exercising every day is his non-negotiable, and he's happier (and healthier!) as a result.

Do you have non-negotiables in your life? What comes to mind with this recommendation? Is there something you know you need, that you know is most important, in this season of your life?

Having one, or a few, clear non-negotiables will help you as you prioritize what matters most and build your life around those priorities.

Share With Others What Matters Most To You

"Action expresses priorities." – Ghandi

Similar to sharing your vision, sharing your top priorities and your non-negotiables often brings others in alignment to help you succeed. When I started a new job and had shared during the interview process that part of the reason I was changing jobs was because I wanted to have a structure where I could be home for dinner with my husband, I was shocked, or perhaps just pleasantly surprised, when my boss was often the one reminding me of that goal – if I was still in the office at 6 p.m., she'd gently ask, "How's it going? What can I do to help you make it home in time for dinner?" Now that my non-negotiable has changed, my husband is my biggest advocate for me creating time to write, and he reminds me – and encourages me – on weekends, and when we are traveling, to build time in for what I say is most important.

You might be thinking that it would be difficult for you to share your non-negotiables with others. Perhaps you don't feel comfortable explicitly sharing your goal, because you don't have a strong relationship with your boss or you're uncertain how it will be received by a friend. In that case, find ways to reinforce it, and in doing so, you'll create the circumstances for success. If it's specific time you block out every day for an activity, put that on your calendar so that no one can book that time with you. By default, you are sharing this priority by not making yourself available, and most of the time people will adapt to the structures you've put in place.

If it is important you will find a way, if not you will find an excuse. How can you find a way to build your life around what matters most to you? Ultimately, prioritizing your life around what matters most will help you live a more fulfilled, meaningful, and optimistic life.

Questions for Reflection:

What's your first answer when you ask yourself what matters most?

Do your actions reflect what is most important to you?

Do you know what your non-negotiables are?

What is a small step you can take to honor your priorities?

CHAPTER 16

LIVE EACH DAY AS THE PERSON YOU'D LIKE TO BECOME

"My life didn't please me. So I created my life."
– Coco Chanel

This Coco Chanel quote accurately and articulately describes where I was a few years ago. I found myself on the brink of being submerged in despair and self-pity, ready to throw in the towel. Exactly what you want to hear from an optimism expert, right? Remember how I said that I started writing this book in one of the most difficult seasons in my life? The beginning of this book was part of my response.

Looking at my glass from an outside perspective, it seemed like my cup was overflowing. I had a great job, I was celebrating eight years of being married to a wonderful man, I had community with family and friends and church and book clubs and non-profits I supported with my time, and lastly, I had a great house in a hip part of town. What more could I ask for? And yet things are never what they seem. My great job was draining the life from me, as I was burnt out, unfulfilled, and dreading going to work each day. My husband and I were going through a tenuous time where connection seemed like a thing of the past, as every day we moved further apart and I couldn't see a light at the end of the tunnel. My community was a solid facade for me going through the motions and putting on the front of a perfect life, but it lacked depth and authentic meaning. My beautiful house felt like a burden each and every day, too, as I was trapped by a mortgage payment and the stress of making ends meet to support this dream. And, to top it all off, my health was suffering as a result of burn-out and stress. Although from the outside my glass was full, from my perspective, the glass was not only bone dry, but I was in the middle of a desert with no way to find water.

Have you found yourself in a moment like this? One where you woke up one day and realized that your life isn't what you thought it would be, and certainly not what you wanted it to be?

During that time, if one more person had told me I just needed to change my perspective, or see the silver lining, or be more grateful, I might have broken the proverbial glass over their head, or thrown it against the wall. Take your pick. Something had to give.

I absolutely agree that, often, a change of perspective, seeing the silver lining, or practicing gratitude can be an important component of being optimistic. But simply how you see something is never as important as what you do with it.

My response to my crisis was a sabbatical. I hit pause. I took a brief leave of absence from my job, I took a break from my marriage, I left my community, I got away from my house, and I moved to Italy for one month. It was my own Under the Tuscan Sun moment. I rented a tiny studio apartment in Bologna, Italy, and I spent thirty days walking through town, thinking, praying, writing, and re-envisioning what my life was going to be like. Reflecting on the life I wanted to create. I had always wanted to be a writer who had the freedom to travel and live abroad, with a fulfilling life based on community created from various places around the world – so I decided to live that, for a brief stint at least.

When I returned from my 1-month sabbatical, of course nothing – as it appeared – had changed. But I had changed. A portion of the change was perspective; as the old adage goes, distance makes the heart grow fonder, and in many cases, the distance I had created gave me an opportunity to reflect on things differently and appreciate things which I had not appreciated in a while. More importantly, my time away had given me the perspective to see where I was selling myself short, and living out of my past and my circumstances, being depleted, instead of living the life I wanted for myself and my future.

I took the same situation that I'd left with one month prior and turned what was a point of observation into a point of action. This was the moment when I decided to change my work situation and leave the job that was burning me out in favor of a job that I found to be more fulfilling. This was the moment when I stopped saying "someday" to my dream of being a writer, and I started writing every day. This was the time when my husband and I tried a number of different things to redefine what we wanted for ourselves and our marriage, and to decide if and how we worked together. This was the time when I restructured my community and surrounded myself with people with whom I could authentically connect with, who understand my multi-passionate and quirky side and don't expect a perfect facade, and who embrace the struggles I was experiencing with my faith and helped me relearn and rebuild what faith meant to me. This was the time when I shifted my attitude towards my home and my mortgage, and found a way to make it an investment that worked for me instead of a burden weighing me down. This was the time when I began viewing self-care as a non-negotiable priority.

I started to not only view myself in the light of the person I wanted to become – a successful entrepreneur and writer who had freedom to travel the world, surrounded by great communities in each location – but I took action to actually create that life and find ways that I could make it my reality. Part of building a new career for myself meant creating space and resources so that I could take time to travel and live abroad. Part of being a writer meant not only saying "someday I'm going to write a book", but actually starting to write every single day and telling other people that I was a writer. Being someone who is blessed by great, dynamic communities meant actually owning the communities I was a part of – whether in Boston, which is my mostly full-time home, or Bologna, Italy where I now spend 4-6 weeks every year. It meant investing in my communities and being authentic and vulnerable with others in order to build the deep and authentic community that I desired. Having an intimate, vibrant, fulfilling marriage meant treating my marriage as if it could be and would be all of those things, but then taking actions that actually reflected that – prioritizing date night, having difficult and uncomfortable conversations, and sacrificing my own ego (a lot).

This didn't all happen overnight – in fact, most of it was four years in the making before I could finally feel like there was some resolution and contentment related to each of these matters, but I feel as though I have finally built the life I want and I am living as if I am already the person I want to become.

Living as the person you'd like to become is critical to living optimistically and looking at yourself optimistically. Not only are you saying "I believe in the best for myself in the future", but you are claiming it now with hope and confidence that you will become the person you are striving for.

You might be wondering, how exactly am I supposed to live as the person I'd like to become? What does that look like? The following tips are the ways I found that work best in living as the person you'd like to become.

How You View Yourself

"You don't become what you want, you become what you believe."
– Oprah Winfrey

Learn to see yourself with fresh eyes. A friend shared this expression with me, and it's stuck with me so much that, a few years ago, it was my resolution and intention for the new year. It's the desire to be seen exactly as you are, in the present moment, with no prior definitions or baggage or expectations. This is the grace that I've learned (and honestly am still learning) to give myself. To accept myself for who I am and where I'm at, with fresh eyes every day. To let whatever mistakes and mishaps occurred previously be things of the past, and to define myself only in the moment of who I am today, and who I'm aspiring to be in all its fullness.

Part of seeing yourself with fresh eyes and viewing yourself truly as the person who you want to become, is claiming who you are. For me, this process meant claiming that I was a writer. Even though it's not my full-time profession, and my first book wasn't published yet when I began expressing this perception, I was a writer by virtue of my action. Seeing myself in this way was a huge step towards actually becoming a writer. For you, perhaps it's being an artist or a musician, or perhaps it's being kind, or adventurous. Viewing yourself as that person you want to be is the first step to actually becoming that person.

How do you view yourself? What would it look like for you to look at yourself with fresh eyes?

How You Treat Yourself

"You are allowed to be both a masterpiece and a work in progress simultaneously." – Sophia Bush

Living each day as the person you want to become is not simply about how you view yourself, but also the way in which you treat yourself. Treat yourself as you would a dear friend. Speak to yourself with love and compassion and belief in your own possibility. Of the three ways to live your life as if you're already the person you want to become, this is the most important one. This is the practical application of belief in your life, and it is the bridge between how you view yourself and the choices you make. In treating yourself like the person you want to become, you are accepting yourself as you are and as the person you aspire to be, and are creating a foundation from which you can become that person.

Do not treat yourself like a failure, beating yourself up and assessing every fault, simply because you have a set-back on your journey. Instead, treat yourself as the work in progress that you are. Recognize the lessons learned and the steps that you can still take forward. Celebrate your accomplishments, no matter how small, and your milestones.

I also recommend looking for small ways to treat yourself in a real, physical, tangible sense, like the person you want to become. For me, I always wanted to live in Paris or Italy. In lieu of that being my present circumstance, I thought about what my life in Paris or Italy would look like, and having amazing coffee every morning was a part of that. So a decade ago I splurged and bought myself an espresso maker so I could make myself a great Italian espresso every morning. Now, I start my days living as if I was in Europe, treating myself to an important component of what life there would be like for me.

What can you do today to treat yourself as a dear friend? To treat yourself to something that embodies the life you want?

The Choices You Make

"I am who I am today because of the choices I made yesterday."
– Eleanor Roosevelt

Ultimately, the way you view yourself and the way you treat yourself needs to translate into the choices you make, these being choices that reflect and embody the person you want to become as if you are already that person. For me, viewing myself as a writer and treating myself as a writer meant – surprise, surprise – actually writing. Beyond the obvious, though, this understanding means consciously choosing to let yourself be who you want to be. If I want to be location independent, and I believe that I can be, I need to start making choices that reinforce that – like taking on projects that allow me to work from anywhere instead of applying for jobs that require me to show up to a specific office every day.

If you aspire to be a rockstar entrepreneur with a thriving business, make choices each day that reflect what you would do if you were that person, if you were thriving in your business and management. Instead of selling yourself short because you are still growing, own the place you want to be with authority and confidence, charge what your services are worth, and guard your time as someone who is succeeding in their own business. If you want to be a better parent, make choices today that reflect what you believe that means, and embrace the actions you can take in the here and now instead of simply saying "someday."

Choosing to live with the hope of becoming who you want to be, and embracing that as part of who you are now, reinforces the optimism with which you view yourself and ultimately the optimism that pours forth from how you live.

Live as though you are already the person you'd like to become, because you are.

Questions for Reflection:

What is your vision for who you want to become?

What would it look like for you to embrace that future version of yourself as part of who you already are?

What choices can you make that reflect hope that you are on the path to becoming who you want to be?

PART 3

LIVING OPTIMISTICALLY

W e started the book with the optimistic mindset, and then moved into the specific and practical arenas in which we can apply optimism in our lives. Now we will discuss the big picture of living optimistically – not the specific steps for one area of our lives, but the ways in which we live our optimism through action and a larger world view.

Ultimately, optimism is not of value unless we do something about it, unless it becomes the lens through which we live our lives and interact with others and the world. Let's revisit our definition of optimism from the beginning of the book:

Optimism is the ability to look at a situation, event, or conditions and believe in the possibility of the most favorable outcomes. It is seeing the good in every situation, believing the best of people and the world, and approaching life with hope and possibility. *Practical optimism* is the ability to see the possibility of the most favorable outcomes, and act in a way that moves toward the most favorable outcome becoming a reality.

Practical optimism is the tangible way in which we live optimistically.

CHAPTER 17

WHAT YOU DO WITH THE GLASS IS MORE IMPORTANT THAN HOW YOU SEE IT

"An optimist is not necessarily someone who looks on the bright side of things, but someone who understands practical ways things can happen." – Kate Chappell

Are you a glass half-full or half-empty sort of person? This seems to be the key question in determining whether someone is an optimist or a pessimist. I believe this question misses the point though. Optimism isn't simply about how you see a situation, or how you see the glass. What you do with the glass is far more important than how you see it. Practical optimism is all about what you do with your glass.

Two days into my college graduation trip to Hawaii, a present from my mom and her best friend, my entire body broke out in rash from the sun and I was instructed to stay indoors for the remainder of our holiday. The hotel doctor suggested that I'd eaten too many Red Vines during finals, and that my body was having an allergic reaction to the red dye in the candy. Needless to say, I spent the remainder of our week on the gorgeous island watching soap operas and reading books. Fast forward a few years, to when my mother and my aunt and I were vacationing in the Caribbean. A few days into our vacation, a similar occurrence happened – a strange rash appeared on my cheek and I was experiencing aches and pains that normally accompany the flu. With the exception of my mother, who is as healthy as can be, the women on my mother's side of the family all suffer from some type of auto-immune disease. My aunt, who was on disability by the time she was 35 due to her illnesses, suggested that I visit the doctor upon my return home and share my specific set of symptoms and family history in order to try and diagnose what was happening.

Since I was a teenager, my body has never seemed to act normally. I've suffered from unusual pain for as long as I can remember, my energy level seems lower and not as high-functioning in comparison to most people my age, I have headaches far more than most, extreme stomach sensitivity, and severe asthma – just to name a few of my health issues. In high school, I went to doctors and physical therapists trying to remedy what was wrong, but I was told time and time again that it was all in my head. As a result, I stopped telling people what was going on. In college and post-college, I learned to be non-committal about all plans because I was never sure how I'd feel, and it was difficult to explain to acquaintances or casual friends why I didn't feel up to going out when nothing was visibly wrong.

Following that trip, I visited a doctor at one of the leading hospitals in Boston – my new hometown. During that first visit, the doctor spent over two hours with me trying to get to the root of the problem, never once suggesting that it was only in my head. Within weeks, I had a name for what I was experiencing – fibromyalgia and early-onset lupus. The relief was palpable – what I had suffered quietly for so long, without explanation, was now defined.

The months that followed were all about learning how to live with my condition. I had to learn how to make wise choices about my diet (anti-inflammatory foods, more veggies, less dairy), lifestyle (stay active, reduce stress as much as possible), living situation (temperate, consistent climates are best), and medicine (enough pills to make me feel like I was 80). Some things were easy to adapt to, but others just didn't fit my life. I'm an event planner – this being consistently ranked one of the top five most stressful jobs ever – so reducing stress while keeping my job was a bit of a joke. And temperate climates? I live in Boston. Not exactly known for moderate, consistent weather. I tried what was suggested whenever possible. Yoga, check. Eight hours of sleep, most of the time. Every medicine recommended, sure.

Years later, on the edge of burn-out and consistently increasing the doses of my medicine to treat my symptoms, my fibromyalgia and lupus symptoms were getting worse – not better. By all accounts, I needed to make some drastic changes to improve my health, and if not, I was going to follow in my aunt's footsteps and be on disability within a few more years. Looking at my glass, I felt that not only was it half-empty, it was unlikely to be refilled.

As part of the recent season of difficulty in my life, I opted to make some drastic changes for my health. Although I am still an event planner, part of my job change was to work for myself in order to create opportunities that help me to manage my stress and prioritize self-care. I found communities for support that helped me learn how to better manage my symptoms, and people who prioritized health and wellness in the ways that I needed to start doing. I worked proactively, and very closely, with my doctors in order to determine a health-care regiment that was right for me. This approach was specific to a long-term plan of wellness, not just treating my symptoms with medicine for a short-term solution. I participated in a study on meditation and the effects of meditation on health and auto-immune disease, and as-a-result, meditation has become one of my daily non-negotiables.

On the surface, my illness and my diagnosis has not changed, nor has the general outcome or suggestions from my doctors. It's still recommended that I don't work as an event planner because it's a high stress job. It's still recommended that I move to a more temperate climate. But that hasn't been practical for me or my life… so despite how I see the glass, what I've done with it is much more important.

"A man full of hope will be full of action." – Thomas Brooks

Whether your glass is half-full, or half-empty, it is not in a permanent state of being. And it's not something that thinking positively in and of itself will change. Regardless of what brought you to this point, you still have the option to choose where to go from here. You can make choices and you can take actions to create change and refill your cup, or share you glass with others, or you can even get more glasses. Okay, I'm overdoing it on the clichés here, but you get my drift.

If you recognize that your current situation is not a permanent state of being, what does it look like for you to take actions to change the state you are in?

The Thomas Brooks quote above reinforces the importance of

action in optimism. It's cyclical, as well. No matter the state of your glass, you can choose to improve it, and in doing so – in taking action to do so – you're exhibiting an expression of hope, an expression of optimism. That expression is contagious, and then creates more opportunities for optimism and hope, and then, by default, more occasions for action.

A big part of deciding what to do with your glass originates with your glass, and taking stock of your glass - your situation. As with meditation, or any traditional Zen thinking, try to take stock without judgment. Observe what is happening. Reflect on what brought you to where you are today. Consider what makes you see the cup as half-empty, or as half-full. Attempt to see things as they are. Not as good or bad; just as a state of being. Once you understand your cup as it is, it's important to understand what fills your cup. What are the things that bring you joy? What would it mean for your cup to be not only full, but overflowing?

Whether you're refilling your own cup, sharing yours with someone else, or trading your cup in entirely, do something. Take action today.

"It isn't what we think that defines us, but what we do."
– Jane Austen

Questions for Reflection:

What are you seeing as half-full today? Half-empty?

What fills your cup? What makes it feel overflowing?

What action can you take today to improve what you have?

CHAPTER 18

CHOOSE ACTION OVER PERFECTION

"Imperfect action is better than perfect inaction."
– Harry Truman

As a full-fledged recovering perfectionist, I have come to believe that perfectionism and optimism often go hand in hand. Not that they always should, but they seem to. When I am in perfectionist mode, I believe that there is a chance for everything to be enhanced, always room for improvement, and often a perfect solution to everything. I used to think that this was actually a good trait – that my striving towards perfection was what allowed me to accomplish so many seemingly great things. I thought that it contributed to my optimism, my ability to see how something could be. But over the past few years, I've realized that it's paralyzed me more than anything.

Do you consider yourself a perfectionist? If not entirely, are there areas of your life where you expect perfection of yourself or of others?

Looking at my childhood, it's easy to see how I would become a perfectionist. I was bullied relentlessly for being different, and I thought, if only I could be perfect like the other kids, then I would be accepted. As a result of being excluded, I would spend my time during recess or after school with the teachers – helping around the classroom, taking on extra projects, or engaging in things that would result in a gold star or recognition for me being a good girl. I spent so much time with my teachers that the principal once called my parents out of concern, stating that I needed to spend more time with my peers. But with the teachers, I was finding acceptance, and the more I found that acceptance the more I thought I needed to perform, perfectly, to ensure that acceptance. So, perfection became my standard.

Until recently, perfection was still how I measured myself. If I could be perfect, or at least give off the impression of being perfect, then I was a success. If not, then I was a failure.

What do you use as a measurement for success in your life? Have you ever fallen into the trap of believing that if something isn't perfect, then it isn't a success?

What I failed to see were the ways in which being perfect prevented me from truly living. I was robbing myself of joy because I was never content with imperfection – and all of life is imperfection. I was creating walls between myself and others because of the value I put on perfection; for one thing, who wants to be friends with someone who presents herself as perfect? And when we expect ourselves to be perfect, it seems as though we expect others to be perfect, as well.

Finally, one day, I realized that I was tired of being perfect. I was tired of waiting 5+ years to start a business simply because I couldn't decide on the perfect business name. The hustle that comes with striving for perfection and yet never attaining it was exhausting. I was weary of being dissatisfied simply because I knew there was a potential for things to be better. The façade of trying to convince everyone I was perfect – which in my line of business is often an expectation – was unsustainable. And I was frustrated with myself for creating an environment of perfectionism to where other people in my life never felt good enough.

So, I became a recovering perfectionist, with this as my new motto: "I hold myself to a standard of grace, not perfection."

Practical optimism requires action, and action cannot exist with perfection. Perfection is unattainable. So, allow yourself to embrace imperfect action in order to move forward.

In the last year that I've been celebrating imperfections, I've found much more joy – and progress – than ever before. It doesn't mean that you should stop striving for greatness. It does mean that you should accept that possibility doesn't require perfection.

"Do not be too timid and squeamish about your actions. All life is an experiment. The more experiments you make the better."
– Ralph Waldo Emerson

Questions for Reflection:

Do you hold yourself to a standard of perfection?

In what ways can you give yourself more grace today?

How can you celebrate your imperfections?

What would less perfection, and more authenticity, look like in your life?

CHAPTER 19

MAKE CHOICES THAT REFLECT HOPE

"Hope transforms pessimism into optimism. Hope is invincible. Hope changes everything. It changes winter into summer, darkness into dawn, descent into ascent, barrenness into creativity, agony into joy. Hope is the sun. It is light. It is passion. It is the fundamental force for life's blossoming." – Daisaku Ikeda

High hopes and low expectations. This is a statement I have never understood, agreed with, or believed. It seems counterintuitive to me – if you have low expectations, then your hopes must not really be high to start. As for me, it's always been a matter of practicing high hopes and high expectations. This can make life with me quite difficult, because it means I am often dealing with disappointment. Regardless of rationality, though, my hopes are always high. And despite the disappointment I am often enduring, I wouldn't have it any other way.

Having hope seems easy in the short term, when we aren't faced with recurring disappointment. Enduring hope that continues even in the face of disappointment is harder to maintain. In what areas of your life are you finding it easy to have high hopes? In what ways is hope feeling impossible?

Hope felt a bit impossible to me a few years ago in the midst of searching for a home. My husband hung up the phone with our realtor as disappointment washed over me. Five years of attempting to buy a house, and eight offers later, including a few for more than asking price and with no contingencies, and still we were being turned away – yet again.

Trying to buy a home in the greater Boston area, and in a competitive market, was not working in our favor. With the first home we decided to pursue, we'd been naively optimistic... we toured the house three separate times, taking entire measurements away to draw up full blueprints of the home, and writing a personalized letter to the sellers about how this would become our family home. We invested blood, sweat and tears into that first offer, only to hear – NO. Yet, we persisted. Each time a new offer came along, we invested as much as we could into making it the best offer, with full belief each time that this was the moment our offer would be accepted. We took steps every day to ensure that we were set up for the mortgage process, that all of our papers were in order for when that next home came about, and we looked relentlessly for open-houses and at new home listings, waiting and choosing to take action that reflected our hope that we would be able to buy a home.

Our 9th offer was the final one. Finally, our five years of making choices that reflected our hope of getting a home paid off. The ironic thing is, despite all the work we put into making choices that reflected our hope – ensuring we had the proper mortgage approval letter for the house, the handwritten letter we wrote to the sellers, the efforts we went to in order to compile all of the research and paperwork required to go through the offer and potential purchase process – I don't think we actually believed that we would get the house. As we walked through the home during an open-house, with dozens of other potential buyers and agents, accompanied by contractors who seemed to carry around briefcases of cash to purchase homes in our neighborhood, we didn't really think or believe that the home would become ours. But we made all the choices that reflected the hope we wanted to have. And much to our shock and surprise, the next day we received the acceptance call. No counter-offer or back-and-forth negotiation… simply a call stating, "Your offer has been accepted!" As we sat stunned by the news, the first question my husband and I pondered was, "Do you remember if the kitchen actually had a fridge?"

"Many of life's failures are people who did not realize how close they were to success when they gave up…. When you have exhausted all possibilities, remember this: you haven't."
– Thomas Edison

In making choices that reflect hope, there is a discipline, a determination, and a faithfulness that comes as part of the process. We don't always feel hope or optimistic in our lives, but we still need to show up as if we do. That is the essence of practical optimism.

Continuing to choose hope – even during trial or difficulty – gives the foundation for that hope and optimism to be realized. Making choices that reflect hope is imperative for it to finally occur in your life.

Questions for Reflection:

Are you choosing hope?

In what ways can you make more choices that reflect hope in your life?

What does it look like for you to have high hopes?

CHAPTER 20

EMBRACE EVERY MOMENT

"Realize deeply that the present moment is all you ever have."
– Eckhart Tolle

One of the common objections I hear about optimism pertains to the bad things that happen in the world and in our lives. I am always being asked, "How can you be optimistic when horrible things are happening?" In the midst of good moments, difficult moments, and moments of in between, being optimistic is about embracing the moment for what it is.

We sat on the stools at the kitchen counter, tears streaming down both of our faces. I put my arm around my brother, as neither of us had words to express the pain we were feeling in the moment. As the older sister, I felt it was my responsibility to find a solution that would fix the difficulty my brother was experiencing. I wanted to say the right thing that would convey that it would all be okay and that everything would work out. But there was nothing to be said. This wasn't one of those moments where a perspective change would fix things, or where a five- step plan would help my brother see more optimistically. This wasn't even a time where I could see optimistically. We were in the middle of one of those moments in life that bring you to your knees, that make you wonder if there is any light or goodness in the world. The moments that shake you at your core. My brother had lost someone he loved. And all I could do was be there, embracing him and the moment as best as possible.

I still well up thinking about that moment, my heart still constricts, and I feel the anguish from that experience as if it were yesterday. As painful as it is to relive that moment, I know that it was one of the most meaningful moments I've experienced in the past year. It was also one of my biggest lessons.

What moment are you facing now that makes optimism seem impossible in your own life? Or in the way that you view others and view the world?

I've prided myself on always being able to be optimistic, always finding the good in a situation, always seeing the light at the end of the tunnel. And yet, here I was, faced with a situation in which optimism was not possible. It was one of those defining moments where I had to reflect on what happens when optimism does not seem like a solution.

Some have asked me to share more details of that moment, and that story, but it's not my story to share. Realistically, the details of my moment with my brother aren't what is important here. Because we all have those moments of difficulty and despair – and those moments will be different for each of us. Perhaps you have lost a loved one. Maybe you are dealing with a health crisis, your own or with someone close to you. The job you once thought was secure might now be non-existent for you or your partner. You may be in despair about the state of our politics, the safety of our children, or the security of the world.

Whatever the circumstances might be, we will all experience moments when it seems impossible to be optimistic.

In that moment with my brother, sitting with discomfort and pain – both over the situation, and also over the realization that optimism might not always be a suitable response – was incredibly difficult and soul-wrenching. In doing so, though, I realized that what I was doing was the optimistic response. I didn't need to fix anything, or change a perspective, or give the tools for how to move forward. No, in this situation, and in many life situations, simply allowing the moment to occur, and embracing it as deeply and authentically as is humanly possible, is the most optimistic thing you can do.

I am all about practical optimism, and about knowing when to take action to make optimism a reality in your life. Yet, I wonder if, on occasion, I use that bias for action as an opportunity to bypass feeling the reality of some of life's ugly, difficult, and painful moments. It is sometimes easier to brush the hurt aside, dust yourself off, and forge forward. And it's entirely likely that, if this situation had been solely about me, I probably would have done just that. But it wasn't about me, and it wasn't my place to forge forward; it was my place to sit and honor the moment, the difficulty, the pain, the hurt, and the uncertainty, as best I could.

Optimism isn't about only seeing the good. It is also about seeing what is, and knowing – even in those dark moments – that a dawn will come. Learning to embrace the darkness, and what it means to be an optimist in the midst of it, has been a lifelong journey for me – and will continue to be a part of my journey.

Life is comprised of so many good and beautiful things, but also hard, ugly, and inexplicable things. Most of life exists in the harmony of it all occurring together – in the ability to experience both joy and sorrow in a single moment, and to see beauty and despair in the same frame.

What are the things defining your life in this moment? The good and beautiful things as well as the hard and ugly things? How does it feel to embrace it all for what it is, experiencing the joy and sorrow in the same moment?

For most of my life, I've seen the world in black and white. Things are good or bad, right or wrong, and answers are yes or no. It impacted how I viewed my life, to the point that I needed everything to be good in order to experience the most joy and fulfillment.

As I've aged – and hopefully matured – I've started to see the nuances of gray. It hasn't been until the last few years that I've embraced the fact that life doesn't exist in the extremes, at the far ends of the spectrum, in the black and white. Life exists everywhere in between, in the messy, unclear, and sometimes indistinct spaces in the middle, in the gray and in the rainbows.

Learning to embrace it all has been the most defining part of my optimism.

Questions for Reflection:

Can you think of the last time you truly embraced a moment, allowing yourself to feel and experience everything to its fullest?

What moments have you missed fully embracing?

What can you do differently today, to embrace every moment?

"Sometimes you will never know the value of a moment until it becomes a memory." – Dr. Seuss

CLOSING

LIFE DOESN'T HAVE TO BE PERFECT TO BE WONDERFUL

"I wanted a perfect ending. Now I've learned, the hard way, that some poems don't rhyme, and some stories don't have a clear beginning, middle, and end. Life is about not knowing, having to change, taking the moment and making the best of it, without knowing what's going to happen next. Delicious Ambiguity."
— Gilda Radner

As I said at the beginning of the book, the irony of the fact that I started writing a book on optimism during one of the most difficult seasons of my life is not lost on me. There is a saying that you teach what you need to learn, and it seems that I needed a reminder about the role of optimism in my life.

My life has been anything but perfect, despite my best attempts to make it so. I have endured struggle and hardship like everyone else. I've succeeded and failed, I've loved and lost, I've soared, and I've fallen hard.

As I write this closing, I am sitting in my 6th floor walk-up apartment in Bologna, Italy, with a grapefruit sized ankle propped up on the edge of the couch and strict orders not to walk for 48-72 hours. This comes after a week of having the flu, during my time in Italy, and being quarantined for seven of the first ten days of my visit here. So, this moment, the here and now, is a very clear example of what I am trying to write about. My life, at this exact moment, is anything but perfect, but it doesn't make it any less wonderful.

Optimism isn't about life being perfect. It is about making the best of where you're at, what you have, who you're with, and where you're going. It's about celebrating, savoring, creating, being, loving, and living. Optimism is the ability to believe in the best possible outcomes, and practical optimism is about acting in ways that make those outcomes your reality.

Optimism is the key to having a more fulfilled, successful, and dynamic life.

Optimism is my superpower. Will you make it yours?

Made in the USA
Columbia, SC
06 August 2018